The Divine Milieu
PIERRE TEILHARD DE CHARDIN

'SIC DEUS DILEXIT MUNDUM'

*For those who love the world**

The Divine Milieu

PIERRE TEILHARD DE CHARDIN

Translated by Siôn Cowell

sussex
ACADEMIC
PRESS

BRIGHTON • PORTLAND

Originally published as *Le milieu divin,* copyright © Editions du Seuil, 1957; published
in the USA by arrangement with HarperCollins Publishers, Inc.; published in this
revised English translation as *The Divine Milieu,* translation/editorial copyright
© 2004 Sussex Academic Press; 'Translator's Note' copyright © 2004
Sussex Academic Press; typeset text, jacket design, index,
copyright © 2004 Sussex Academic Press

The right of Siôn Cowell to be identified as editor and translator of this work has been
asserted in accordance with the Copyright, Designs and Patents Act 1988.

2 4 6 8 10 9 7 5 3 1

First published 2004 in hardcover, in Great Britain by
SUSSEX ACADEMIC PRESS
Box 2950
Brighton BN2 5SP

and in the United States of America by
SUSSEX ACADEMIC PRESS
920 NE 58th Ave   Suite 300
Portland, Oregon 97213-3786

British Library Cataloguing in Publication Data
A CIP catalogue record for this book is available from the British Library.

Library of Congress Cataloging-in-Publication Data
Teilhard de Chardin, Pierre.
  Milieu divin. English
  The divine milieu / Pierre Teilhard de Chardin ; in a revised
translation by Siôn Cowell.
    p. cm.
  Includes index.
  ISBN 1-903900-58-1 (alk. paper)
  1. Christianity—Philosophy. I. Cowell, Siôn. II. Title.
BR100 .T373 2003
233—dc21
                                            2003012806
                                                  CIP

The frontispiece of Pierre Teilhard de Chardin is an original portrait by Caroline Cowell,
painted in oils, 1993; original size 55 × 60 cm.

Typeset and designed by G&G Editorial, Brighton
Printed in the UK by The Cromwell Press, Trowbridge, Wiltshire.
This book is printed on acid-free paper.

CONTENTS

CONCLUSION TO PARTS ONE AND TWO
General Remarks on Christian Asceticism

PART THREE
The Divine Milieu

EPILOGUE

FOREWORD BY THOMAS M. KING SJ

In the Autumn of 1914 German armies invaded France, by Christmas they were approaching Paris. Pierre Teilhard de Chardin, a Jesuit priest studying geology at the University of Paris, was found fit for military service and drafted into the French army. Given three weeks of training, on January 21, 1915 he was sent to the front lines of World War I. Though offered a commission, he preferred to stay with the other draftees and serve as a stretcher bearer with a regiment of North African light infantry. He took part in many major battles of the war (Ieper [Ypres], Arras, Douaumont, Louvemont, and so forth), and was cited as a 'model of bravery, self-sacrifice, and coolness'. He was given the Croix de Guerre and the Military Medal and made a Chevalier in the Legion of Honor. A fellow soldier, Max Bégouën, wrote of him:

> 'The North African sharpshooters of his regiment thought he was protected by his *baraka*.[1] The curtain of machine gun fire and the hail of bombardments both seemed to pass him by. During the attacks of September 25 at Artois, my brother was wounded, and, as he wandered on the battlefield, he saw a single stretcher bearer rising up in front of him, and he, for it was Teilhard, accomplished his mission quite imperturbably under terrible fire . . . "I thought I had seen the appearance of a messenger from God."
>
> 'I once asked Father Teilhard, "What do you do to keep this sense

[1] *Baraka*: an Arabic word meaning 'spiritual stature' or 'supernatural quality'.

of calm during the battle? It looks as if you do not see the danger and that fear does not touch you."

'He answered, with that serious but friendly smile which gave such a human warmth to his words, "If I'm killed I shall just change my state, that's all."'[2]

It was between the battles of war that Teilhard began to develop the basic lines of his vision; to clarify his thoughts and leave a witness of what he saw; he began writing a series of essays that would later make him famous. After the War, he would refine and clarify his ideas, but they remained the basic insights he developed amidst the horrors of trench warfare. 'The War was the springtime of my ideas—my intellectual honeymoon.'[3]

Teilhard was born in central France on May 1, 1881, the fourth of eleven children. His family was part of the local gentry and hired German and English tutors for the education of the children. But his mother reserved the teaching of religion to herself; she was a devout lady who gathered the family and servants each evening for common prayer. Pierre's father was a gentleman farmer with an interest in Natural History; he took the children on long walks and identified for them the fauna, the flora, the stars, and—for Pierre—the rocks. Pierre shared in the deep faith of his mother, but at six or seven he had another interest: he was drawn to Matter. He began collecting small scraps of iron: part of a plough, an hexagonal bolt, and shell casings from a neighboring firing range. He called them his 'God of Iron,' and explained that in all his childish experience he found nothing harder and more durable than that wonderful substance.

Upon discovering that iron rusts and can be scratched, he threw himself down on the lawn weeping in childish despair. Soon he was looking for substitutes that would console him; for a short while it was the quartz and chalcedony found in the region. But the hardest of rocks can break, so he turned his attention to the earth itself, for the ultimate matter of earth seemed to be the true indestructible. He

[2] Nicolas Corte, *Pierre Teilhard de Chardin* (New York: Macmillan, 1960), p. 15.
[3] *Letters to Léontine Zanta* (London: Collins, 1969), p. 52.

would speak of this interest as a love for the universe, and tell of a cosmic sense, a sense of plenitude that drew him to the All (*le Tout*).

When Pierre was ten, his mother brought him to the Jesuit boarding school at Mongré. There he was 'disconcertingly well-behaved' and won many academic honors—only one was in religion. As graduation approached he wrote to his family, 'God is offering me a vocation to leave the world.' This was his way of saying he would renounce his interest in the rocks and enter the Jesuits. But upon graduation from the Jesuit college, he looked so weak that his father made him wait a year. On March 20, 1899 he entered the Jesuit novitiate at Aix-en-Provence. 'It was a desire for what was most perfect that made me enter the Jesuits.' Yet the rocks continued to fascinate him: 'The fire is still in me more active than ever.' Fellow novices tell of 'Brother Teilhard' never going for a walk without his geological hammer and magnifying lens. But this interest began interfering with his prayer, so he went to his novice director and proposed that he renounce geology and concentrate on studies for the priesthood. The novice director assured him that the natural development of his mind was also the will of God, so he came out of his novice-director's door feeling he was holding two ends of string; they were pulling him in opposite directions, God and the material world. Only gradually did he see how the two attractions support one another.

Following his novitiate, Teilhard studied Latin, Greek, and Philosophy in a Jesuit seminary in Jersey, a British island off the coast of France. Then in 1905 he was sent to teach chemistry and physics at the Jesuit college in Cairo. While in Jersey and Egypt he continued his interest in geology and began publishing what he found. He was fascinated by the rocks around Cairo and in El Fayum: 'This was the East. I caught glimpses of it, and drank it in avidly, with no concern for its peoples and their history . . . but under the attraction of its light, its vegetation, its fauna and its deserts.'[4] All the while, a voice seemed to whisper in his ear, 'Why should I not look for the essence

[4] 'The Heart of Matter,' in *The Heart of Matter* (London: Collins; New York: Harcourt Brace Jovanovich, 1978), p. 23.

of Matter, for its "heart," precisely in the direction in which all things are "ultra-materialized?"' That led him to believe, 'If I was to be All, I must be fused with All.'[5] In short, in 1908 he was in a 'somewhat muddled spiritual complex' as he left Cairo to continue studies for the priesthood at the Jesuit Theologate at Hastings in England.

While studying Theology, Teilhard again used his free-time to study the geology of the region. This led him to an unfortunate involvement. While he and a fellow Jesuit were exploring a local quarry, another amateur geologist, Charles Dawson, approached them. Dawson soon was to become the central figure in what now is known as the 'Piltdown hoax'. This refers to nine pieces of a human skull and the jawbone of an orangutan that had been doctored to look ancient and as if they belonged to the same individual. On two occasions Teilhard assisted Dawson in digging at the site. In December 1912, Piltdown materials were presented to the scientific world and were widely acclaimed. They continued to fool anthropologists until 1953 when modern research techniques showed they had been artificially prepared. In 1980 Stephen Jay Gould, a Harvard anthropologist and TV personality, accused Teilhard of involvement in producing the fraud, a charge that has been abundantly repeated and abundantly refuted.[6] But Gould was a popular writer and his charge has left a shadow on Teilhard's name.

---

[5] *Ibid.*, p. 24.

[6] For many years Stephen Jay Gould wrote a monthly column in *Natural History*. In August of 1980, his column accused Teilhard of complicity in preparing the hoax. Many scholars have taken issue with Gould: J. S. Weiner, who led in uncovering the fraud and later published *The Piltdown Forgery* (Oxford, 1955), claimed Dawson was the forger but allowed there might have been an accomplice. Weiner had interviewed Teilhard in 1954 for about an hour concerning his memories of Piltdown. In 1981 Weiner spoke at Georgetown University dismissing Gould's charge as 'rubbish': 'I had no reason then and I have no reason now—I have said so in public many times—to see in Teilhard a fellow conspirator' (a video of this talk is available in the Georgetown University archives). Together with Weiner the present author has written a defense of Teilhard that appeared in *Teilhard & the Unity of Knowledge* (Paulist, 1983). Kenneth Oakley, Weiner's associate in uncovering the fraud said the basis of Gould's charge is 'completely untrue.' Teilhard was involved with Piltdown, but, like many other anthropologists, he was an early victim of the fraud, not a conspirator. Many scholars have defended Teilhard's innocence. The best defense would seem to be articles by Tobias

While at Hastings Teilhard read Henri Bergson's *Creative Evolution*, and found it to be fuel for a fire that was already consuming his heart and mind.[7] Now his smoldering sense for the All burst into flame. But the All had changed; the All was in process; he knew it as a presence, 'a profound, ontological, total drift of the Universe'; all things were 'evolving'. The word evolution began haunting his mind like a tune, like a summons. The world around him seemed to be moving with a single life. At sunset the English countryside appeared charged with the same fossil life he was pursuing in rocky cliffs and quarries. 'There were moments when it seemed to me that a sort of universal being was about to take shape suddenly in Nature before my very eyes.'[8]

Teilhard was ordained a priest in August 1911, and in the following year Jesuit superiors sent him to study geology at the University of Paris. Marcellin Boule, a fellow Auvergnat and specialist in the Neanderthals, became his mentor. Boule was known to be anti-clerical, but from their first meeting they liked one another and eventually Boule wanted Teilhard to replace him at the Paris Museum. But before Teilhard could complete his studies, he was drafted into the army and sent to the Front. Between battles he began coming to understand how the transcendent, personal God of Revelation might relate to the impersonal All. He saw evolution as the rising of the All into consciousness, and, appealing to texts from S. Paul, he saw the transcendent God descending into the earth. God and the material world were uniting to form the Body of Christ. He began seeing the events of his time as leading to a unified world with Christ as its Soul.

---

and Kennedy that appeared in *Current Anthropology* (June 1992 and February 1993). See also Charles Blinderman, *The Piltdown Inquest* (Prometheus, 1986) and James E. Walsh, *Unraveling Piltdown* (Random House, 1996). Recent evidence indicates Martin Hinton, a worker at the British Museum and much involved with the Piltdown finds, prepared the fraud. The evidence is a trunk with Hinton's initials recently found in the attic of the British Museum containing fossils stained by the same complex process used on the Piltdown materials (*Nature*, April 23, 1996).

[7] 'The Heart of Matter', p. 25.

[8] *Ibid.*, p. 26.

Teilhard believed other Christians were puzzled by the same two attractions that he had known, God and the World. He often wrote of them as two Stars dividing our allegiance. The First Chapter of *The Divine Milieu* is an attempt to show how these two Stars come into conjunction. The result is that, if human work is done with the right intention, it can be rendered holy, because of what it achieves, the Body of Christ. By his studies in Geology and Theology, he saw the Stars coming together.[9] The rising earth would provide the Body for which Christ would be the Soul. And ordinary human work contributes to the process; it provides a suitable Body.

Teilhard tried to bring his message down to earth and into the lives of ordinary people. He wrote to a friend whose business affairs were prospering:

> 'You are still having some difficulty in justifying to yourself the euphoria of a soul immersed in "business". I must point out to you that the really important thing is that you are actually experiencing that feeling of well-being. Bread was good for our bodies before we knew about the chemical laws of assimilation. . . . How, you ask, can the success of a commercial enterprise bring with it moral progress? And I answer in this way, that, since everything in the world follows the road to unification, the spiritual success of the universe is bound up with the correct functioning of every zone of that universe and particularly with the release of every possible energy in it. Because your enterprise (which I take to be legitimate) is going well, a little more health is being spread in the human mass, and in consequence a little more liberty to act, to think, and to love . . . '

Behind what he writes is the understanding that as the world becomes more organically one, it forms a more suitable Body for Christ.

As the First World War came to a close, Teilhard was calling for 'planetization'—today we would speak of 'globalization'. He saw the world becoming increasingly one world as nations came together, even through the tragedies of war. He would write in favor of the

---

[9] During this time he developed a vision of how the two attractions might relate:

League of Nations and later for the United Nations. For he would claim, 'The Age of Nations is past. The task before us now, if we do not wish to perish, is to shake off our ancient prejudices and build the Earth.'[10] Building the earth is the basic message for which Teilhard has become known. Many concerned with the international have appealed to Teilhard: U Thant, former Secretary General of the United Nations, was concerned lest the UN become simply a forum where grievances were aired. So he had the UN sponsor two symposia on the thought of Teilhard. For the texts of Teilhard seemed to best express his vision of what the UN could be. Michel Camdessus, Director of the International Monetary Fund for thirteen years, frequently cited Teilhard to tell of his work: 'A formidable

1. Through a scientific study of the material world Teilhard learned of the evolution of life. He saw the material world building up increasingly complex structures. And with the build up of the earth there was a corresponding growth in the psyches of the living. As life proceeded through fish, reptiles, mammals and primates to the human, living organisms became increasingly conscious. Thus, experience testifies that over the millennia the physical world has been 'complexifying' and matter is rising in spirit.

2. Through a spiritual study of the Revelation, Teilhard learned that the personal and transcendent God had entered the world of matter, the New Testament tells of God's descent into the lowest parts of the earth so that rising from there he might fill all things (Eph 4:10). Christ is progressively drawing all things into himself to become the one in whom 'all things hold together' (Col 1:17). The Body of Christ would one day include all things.

Thus, the Two Stars are in process of coming together. Through the ascent of matter and the descent of God. The impersonal cosmos (the Body) and the personal God (the Soul) are uniting to form the Body of Christ. Eventually the world will have a single Soul.

In today's world Teilhard saw peoples and nations becoming increasingly interrelated—as if to form a single common organism. Other writers have told of the organic unity of the earth (Julian Huxley, Lewis Thomas, James Lovelock). But Teilhard understood this growing organic unity to be the Body of Christ in process of formation. Thus, the rise and spread of the living, the scientific and economic development of the earth, and the human efforts to build a society of love, justice, and understanding are all parts of a single cosmic process—the process by which Christ is forming his Body. Those who realize the sacred work in which they are involved will no longer feel lost in cosmic immensities. They will see that the least of their activities can be a communion with God. To realize this communion, Teilhard would urge that we become aware of our roots in ages past. Then, aware of the cosmic movement of which we are part, we will sense our final destiny in God.

10 'Spirit of the Earth', 1931, in *Human Energy* (London: Collins, 1969), pp. 37–38.

dignity is found in this work in which God and Man join hands and which makes our History a Holy History.' He claimed the texts of Teilhard were on his mind every day during his years at the IMF. Léopold Senghor, longtime president of Senegal, saw Teilhard offering an alternative to Marxism and the vision Africa needed as it moved beyond its colonial past. When Senghor made a state visit to the US, he began by praying at the tomb of Teilhard in Poughkeepsie, New York. This international vision was much on the mind of Teilhard as the First World War came to an end, and it is the message of the First Chapter of *The Divine Milieu*. There human action is divinized as it renders the earth more organically one, and that brings Christ's Body closer to its completion.

The Second Chapter has a different message. It is not concerned with the things we do, but with that which happens to us. As a soldier Teilhard could not follow his own will; in a fundamental sense, he was passive, yet the War was a time of growth for Teilhard. At the same time he saw diminishments in the bodies of soldiers that he carried back, some missing a limb, some living and some dead. Two of his brothers died in the War. A close Jesuit friend of Teilhard, and author of many studies of his thought, Henri de Lubac, claimed that all the writings of Teilhard are one long meditation on death. During the War he wrote, 'The universe assumes the form of Christ—but, O mystery! the one we see is the Christ crucified.'[11] Many who resonate to the positive message of Teilhard have overlooked his awareness of human helplessness. But he also knew of a helplessness that is built into the universe. As a student of physics he learned of entropy; that is, the structures of the universe are wearing down and after several billions of years the universe will descend into chaos. Then one can ask, 'If all things lead to an inevitable death, what is the point of human labor? Of building a better world?' Here his answer was specifically Christian.[12] He looked at a battlefield strewn with

[11] The Priest,' in *Writings in Time of War* (London: Collins; New York: Harper & Row, 1968), p. 208.
[12] Letter to Marguerite Teillard-Chambon, August 23, 1916, in *The Making of a Mind* (London: Collins; New York: Harper & Row, 1965), p. 119.

bodies and said, 'Only the image of the crucified can sum up, express and relieve all the horror, and beauty, all the hope and deep mystery in such an avalanche of conflict and sorrow.'

When Teilhard was demobilized in March of 1919, he returned to Paris to continue his doctoral studies. In 1922 he completed these with distinction and was appointed assistant professor in Geology at the Catholic Institute. He had wanted a position more adventure-some ('I should have preferred research work in Beirut, or Shanghai, or Trichinopoly'). The adventures soon came: A fellow Jesuit, Fr. Émile Licent, had been working as a scholar and missionary in China. He began finding significant fossils and some early human tools in Mongolia and sent them back to the Paris Museum of Natural History. To appraise the materials and continue the exploration, Teilhard went to China to work with Licent. In the summers of 1923 and 1924, the two went into the Ordos where they found a rich trove of fossils and additional tools left by early humans.

Teilhard returned to France in the Fall of 1924 and soon found he was in trouble with the Church authorities. For, while he was in China, someone took an essay on Original Sin from his desk at the Catholic Institute and sent it to Rome. The essay claimed that the story of Adam and Eve should be understood as a parable and not as early human history. (A position widely held by Catholic theologians today, but not held widely or openly at the time.) Besides that, some of his earlier writings continued to circulate and some passages had seemed pantheistic. He was obliged to sign a statement affirming he would not write things apart from the Catholic tradition on Original Sin and was told he could no longer teach at the Catholic Institute. No restrictions were placed on his scientific writing, but he was not allowed to publish writings in philosophy or theology without Vatican approval. In Paris, he had become a popular speaker—especially among younger clergy—so to diminish his influence it was decided that he should return to China and continue his scientific work.

Teilhard resumed work in China in the Spring of 1926. But he also began planning a devotional book that he hoped would help others

live the faith and show his orthodoxy. In November 1926 he wrote
to a friend:

> 'I want to set down as simply as possible the sort of ascetical and
> mystical doctrine that I have been living and preaching so long. I call
> it *The Divine Milieu*. . . . I really mean to try to "get across" and to have
> the book read. I think that if I could manage to get it printed, it would
> do good in two ways: it would spread ideas which I believe would
> open new frontiers for many minds, and at the same time my efforts
> might be rewarded by some kind of approval from the Church. I have
> settled down to my little book. I want to write it slowly, quietly, living
> it, and meditating on it like a prayer.'[13]

As the writing proceeded he spoke of it as 'more balanced than
anything I have written'. He completed the text in March of 1927 and
sent it out to censors seeking approval. Several small changes were
proposed and he had no trouble in accepting them. Arrangements
were made for publishing it at Leuven [Louvain] in Belgium. But
someone in the Vatican expressed concern and Leuven decided not
to proceed. 'A pity that everything is held up through intervention
from Rome.' He felt helpless. His message had appealed to believers
and non-believers; he knew many hesitant Christians found their
faith was renewed in hearing his words, but the Church he defended
so ardently was reluctant to allow his influence to increase. He would
have to live with this restriction for the rest of his life.

As a scientist, Teilhard's work went well and he traveled often
between China, Paris, and the US. He worked in excavations in India,
Burma and Java, but most of his scientific work was centered in China
where he was geologist for the excavations at Choukoutien
[Zhoukoudian] in which the fossil skulls of Peking Man were
found—the first skull was found in December 1929. Choukoutien
was a hill about 50 kilometers (30 miles) southwest of Peking
[Beijing]; Peking Man was then known as the first fire-user and lived
bout 400,000 years ago. In 1930, Teilhard joined the American adven-
turer, Roy Chapman Andrews, on an expedition into Mongolia. In

[13] Robert Speaight, *Teilhard de Chardin* (London: Collins, 1967), p. 143.

his official account of the expedition Andrews wrote, 'We were delighted to have Father Teilhard as a colleague because of his brilliant achievements and his charming personality endeared him to all of us.'[14] Secular scientists were taken by the man and his scientific work without necessarily accepting his religious message: George Gaylord Simpson found him 'extraordinarily likable, with an indescribably warm and sparkling personality combined with an attractive humility on every subject but one'. The 'one' is the physical presence of Christ in the universe! Jia Lanpo [Chia Lan-po], a Chinese archaeologist, met Teilhard when he was a young student of anthropology. In 1981, he reflected: 'This scientist of towering stature quickly put me at ease with his amicable manner and his tirelessness in educating the young learner.'[15] Jia tells of difficulties associated with the work and adds: It was 'a moving experience to see how many hardships the man could bear.'[16] Expeditions took him to difficult areas where he endured blistering heat, icy blizzards, poor food, sandstorms, snakes, flash floods, marauding bandits, civil war, political intrigue, bribery, and maddening policy changes leveled by unstable governments. In May 1931 he set out across central Asia in a large ten-month expedition sponsored by the Citroen Corporation. He was the only practicing Catholic, and found it difficult to make his usual hour of meditation, but found compensation in 'the treasures of friendship'. When one of the party expressed his doubts about the existence of God, Teilhard replied in a casual tone, 'God is a choice; a very simple choice; the choice between a yes and a no, between the plus sign and the minus sign. None of us can avoid making this choice, and it is extremely difficult to make the wrong one.'[17]

Teilhard wrote many accounts of his scientific findings; these were published in scientific journals. The articles have been collected

[14] Roy Chapman Andrews, *The New Conquest of Central Asia* (New York: American Museum of Natural History, 1932), Vol. I, p. 422.
[15] Jia Lanpo and Huang Woiwen, *The Story of Peking Man: From Archaeology to Mystery*, trans. Yin Zhiqi (New York and London: Oxford University Press), p. 240.
[16] *Ibid.*, p. 251.
[17] Speaight, *Teilhard de Chardin*, p. 182.

in ten large volumes. He also continued writing philosophic and religious articles, hoping they could eventually be published. Most of these were published only after he died; now they form a collection of thirteen volumes. A dozen collections of his letters have been published as well as one volume of his Journal of Ideas. His scientific writings gave him an international standing. But he could not freely proclaim or publish the religious message that was central to his thoughts. In the scientific world he was a success, but his fellow Jesuits tell of him weeping with his head on his knees, because he could not speak freely of what concerned him.

Teilhard read the English astronomer, James Jeans. Jeans, like Teilhard, was aware that entropy would overtake the universe and eventually all things would die. Still Jeans claimed that with luck the human adventure on earth could last for millions and millions of years. Teilhard found Jeans offering the antithesis of his own thought, for Jeans still spoke of an eventual disintegration. For Teilhard this was not enough, for he believed humans will act only if they know there is something that will endure forever, and that means beyond the present universe.[18] He spoke many times of life after death. If this were not the case he saw the whole of evolution to be without meaning. Events led him to reflect on this:

A Canadian named Davidson Black was director of the excavations at Choukoutien. He was known to have heart problems, but seemed to be doing well. Yet on March 16, 1934, his fellow workers found him lying dead beside his desk in the laboratory. Teilhard reflected:

'But what an absurd thing life is, looked at superficially, so absurd that you feel yourself forced back on a stubborn, desperate, faith in the reality and survival of the spirit. Otherwise—were there no such thing as the spirit, I mean—we should have to be idiots not to call off the whole human effort . . .'[19]

'Black was the companion of my mind and heart, and it was with

---

[18] Cf. *Letters from a Traveler* (London: Fontana, 1967), p. 131.
[19] Letter to Rev. Henri Breuil, March 18, 1934, *ibid.*, p. 155.

him that I envisaged my work. But there is more in it than that. I mean a sharp concrete "realization" of the utter vanity of "human effort" unless there is both a natural and supernatural emergence of the universe towards some immortal consciousness. In my distress following Black's death, and in the stifling atmosphere of "agnostic" condolences that surrounded it, I swore to myself, on the body of my dead friend, to fight more vigorously than ever to give hope to human work and inquiry.'[20]

To give humans hope Teilhard began writing his best known work, *The Human Phenomenon*, in 1938. He interrupted his writing to go to Paris by way of the United States. In Paris he was offered a position in the Institute of Human Paleontology—afraid that this honor might give weight to his religious message, the Roman authorities delayed eight months before allowing him to take up the position. While in Paris, he met a woman named Jeanne Mortier who had read a 'samizdat' copy of *The Divine Milieu* and was taken by the message. She volunteered to serve as his secretary, and he entrusted to her copies of his many works. She began producing roneotype copies of his essays (Church restrictions forbid him to have his works printed) and sending them to interested parties. He returned to China arriving in September 1939, just as World War Two was beginning in Europe. He soon settled in to work seriously on *The Human Phenomenon*. There he told of the phases of evolving life, arguing that evolution has a direction (a controverted position), and the direction was towards forms of increased consciousness. Then, using the past to foretell the future, he argued that the nations were coming together to form a united humanity. He completed the work on June 18, 1940, the very day the French surrendered to the Nazi invaders. The work tells of a bright future with a united humanity animated by God. But events in Europe seemed to contradict all he wrote, and around him the Japanese continued a cruel occupation of Peking. He sustained a group of friends with his hopeful message, yet, he was troubled within. He

[20] Letter to Max-Henri and Simone Bégouën, April 10, 1934, *ibid.*, pp. 155–56.

began suffering from periods of 'nervous depression'. During the War the foreign community in Peking was greatly restricted, friends disappeared without notice, and life was austere. Teilhard joked, 'We have no trouble with mice in our house; for we have nothing to eat.' When the War ended, Teilhard began making arrangements to return to Paris. He arrived there in May of 1946 to find he had become famous. Jeanne Mortier had been reproducing his essays and sending them to those interested.

The Second Chapter of *The Divine Milieu* concerns human passivities. In the First World War Teilhard had faced the possibility of death every day; after the War he found himself helpless and unable to speak because of restrictions placed on him by the Church he loved. But human passivities were deeper than this. All of us were passive through the long ages in which the human genome was developed, passive as we were formed in the womb, and passive as our body grew—our passivities are 'immeasurably wider and deeper' than our activities.[21] We were passive as the forces of evolution brought us to life and growth, and passive as the same forces draw us to diminishment and death. Our conscious minds are the peak of what evolution has produced. The whole of evolution will be without meaning if its finest product, the human mind, must end in death. So Teilhard saw death as the great moment of Communion with the God who transcends this world.

A trust that God will lead us beyond the present life emerges from the Second Chapter of *The Divine Milieu*. The Chapter concerns human passivities. Even our own minds seem to act in ways we do not intend. 'My self is given to me far more than it is formed by me.'[22] In the end, each of us sinks into the total passivity of death. So the Second Chapter tells of the meaning of the Cross: 'In its highest and most general sense, the doctrine of the Cross is what all adhere to who believe that the vast movement and agitation of human life opens on to a road which leads somewhere.'[23] His message is for 'all

[21] Cf. *The Divine Milieu*, p. 36.
[22] *Ibid.*, p. 38.
[23] *Ibid.*, p. 62.

people', Christians and others. For to believe that the whole of evolution is going anywhere, one must believe life has its completion beyond physical death. All about us we see people striving to rise into the fullness of life, and whether they are more or less successful or if they are dogged by failure, they are equally subject to suffering and death. If such striving has any meaning, it can only be in a reality beyond the phenomena. This is the mystery of the Cross. In 1948, Teilhard returned to *The Human Phenomenon* to add a brief section on the reality of evil and suffering. Now, the text ends with the line: 'Even in the eyes of a mere biologist, it is still true that nothing resembles the way of the Cross as much as the human epic.'[24]

Back in Paris after the Second World War, Teilhard found many responding to his ideas, but the Church authorities would not allow him to publish or speak to large gatherings. One account tells of his going to give a scheduled talk, but, finding a large crowd present, he decided not to speak. He could no longer be sent into exile in China, as China had become Communist and was not welcoming back Christian missionaries. However, he was aware that since 1924 significant human fossils were being found in South Africa and Rhodesia that seemed to indicate the human race originated in Africa. So in 1947, Teilhard was planning a trip to the fossil sites in South Africa, when he was struck by a major coronary and for ten days hovered between life and death. After a long period of convalescence, he slowly returned to work. He was able to travel to the US in February 1948 and visit friends and scientific associates. He continued to be plagued by periods of nervous anxiety. A close Jesuit friend, Pierre Leroy, who worked with him many years in Peking, tells of assisting him shortly after his return to France in the summer of 1948:

> 'When the dinner hour came, he refused to leave his room. He begged me not to leave him, and I tried, without success, to comfort him. Finally I remembered one of his remarks he himself had made to others when they were in great pain. Placing his crucifix before him, I reminded him that the cross was not empty, but that the image of

[24] *The Human Phenomenon* (Brighton & Portland: Sussex Academic Press, 1999), p. 226

the God-Man was there. He returned to me a look so sorrowful that
I automatically took him into my arms, if only to give him a little
human warmth.'[25]

Teilhard traveled to Rome hoping to get permission to publish *The
Human Phenomenon* and accept a chair in science at the College of
France. But he was refused on both accounts. 'Those people in Rome
are living on another planet.' Back in Paris he urged Jeanne Mortier
to continue her work reproducing his essays and saving them for the
future. People he did not know sought him out and he knew his
message was getting out and awakening enthusiasm. When he heard
the French bishops were planning on complaining to Rome about
his activities, he decided, with the encouragement of his Jesuit superiors, he would do well to leave Paris for a while. He sought the
financial support of Paul Fejos of the Wenner-Gren Foundation to
make the trip to South Africa he had not been able to make earlier.
But, before he left and at the encouragement of his acting Rector, he
turned over the rights to his manuscripts to Jeanne Mortier. It was
she who made arrangements for their publication after his death.

After his coronary in 1947, he was no longer able to get around as
before. The Jesuit authorities gave him permission to have an
American woman (Rhoda de Terra) accompany him. In South Africa,
he traveled to sites where early human fossils had been found and
soon affirmed that the human race originated in Africa—not in Asia
as had been generally believed. In doing field work his spirits were
revived. After two months of traveling to different excavations, he
left for America. There he stayed at St. Ignatius' Church as he wrote
up his report for Wenner-Gren; but after that his position was uncertain. He wrote to the General of the Jesuits trying to explain himself,
'You must resign yourself to taking me as I am.' He tells briefly of his
vision of the universe converging on Christ and of feeling more indis-
solubly bound to the hierarchical Church and the Christ of the
Gospel than ever before. But the point of the letter is to assure the
General, that in spite of any apparent evidence to the contrary, 'I am

---

[25] *Letters from My Friend Teilhard de Chardin* (New York: Paulist, 1980), p. 27.

resolved to remain a "child of obedience."' He explained, 'What might have been taken in my attitude during the last thirty years for obstinacy or disrespect, is simply the result of my absolute inability to contain my own feeling of wonderment.'

A feeling of wonderment runs through the Third Chapter of *The Divine Milieu* giving it an intuitive character that leaves many passages difficult to understand. There he tells of feeling like he has entered a new realm—he is living now in the Divine Milieu. He cannot say when it began, but everything around him had taken on a radiance and every act has become a moment of Communion. But with the change he still had his day-to-day difficulties and still suffered from times of depression. Like other mystics, he would know both the agony and the ecstasy. He had many old friends in New York and made many new ones, and with them he had an active social life in which he presented what he saw. In 1953 he traveled again to South Africa again and again Rhoda had to assist him in making travel arrangements, getting the proper vaccination shots, and trying to clarify his US visa. Shortly after his return he was disappointed to hear that the Piltdown fossils had been faked and he had been duped. In 1954 he was given permission to visit France; he visited his family in the Auvergne and scientific associates in Paris, but, because of the commotion he was causing in Paris, his Jesuit superiors requested that he leave early. Back in New York the Jesuits were repairing their residence, so with the permission of the Jesuit Provincial, he was able to stay in the apartment of a friend at the Lotus Club, a place 'strictly cloistered'. He shared the apartment with Fr. Emmanuel de Breuvery who worked at the United Nations. Fr. Leroy was working on a research project in Chicago and tells of seeing him one final time:

'The last time I saw Teilhard was in New York a few days before Christmas, 1954. I found him weaker and harassed. Little did I know that I was never to see him again alive. One day we were going to a restaurant for lunch. We were walking the streets of New York. All of a sudden he stopped, put his hand on my shoulder, looked at me intensely, and he spoke a testament as he said: "Now I think I can tell you. I am living continuously in the presence of God." Just in those streets of New York. Imagine!'[26]

During the Lenten season he seemed more restless than ever. He daily offered Mass at the Dominican Church of St. Vincent Ferrer. He did desk work at the Wenner-Gren and returned each night to the men's club where he lived and tried to express with greater precision what he feared only a few would read. In one of these essays, he said he wanted to present one final time the same fundamental vision that he first presented 40 years earlier. He looked back on *The Divine Milieu* and saw it as an earlier attempt 'to give distinct expression to my wonder and amazement'. Now, in feeling his age, he feared he could not express it with the same freshness and enthusiasm, 'but,' he added, 'the wonder and the passion will still be there, undimmed'. He sent the essay to Jeanne Mortier not knowing if more than a few people would read it. On Holy Saturday, he and Fr. de Breuvery made their confessions to one another. On Easter Sunday, April 10, he said a private Mass and then went to St. Patrick's cathedral for a Solemn Mass. After Mass he met Rhoda de Terra and her daughter and together they attended a concert. He complained of not feeling well, so they left early and went to her home where she began preparing dinner. He was talking with her daughter, when suddenly he fell full length on the floor. For a brief moment, he seemed to regain consciousness and asked, 'Where am I? What happened.' He was assured he was with friends. Within minutes he had died of a cerebral hemorrhage.

On Tuesday he was buried from St. Ignatius' Church on Park Avenue and only a handful of mourners were present. His body was driven up the Hudson to the Jesuit cemetery in Poughkeepsie, New York. *The New York Times* carried his obituary. It told of his scientific work and called him a priest who saw evolution consonant with his Christian faith, but made no mention of the explanations he had offered. For his religious and philosophic writings remained unpub-

---

[26] Pierre Leroy, Talk at Georgetown University, May 1987.

lished in the filing cabinet of Jeanne Mortier. Hearing of his death, she proceeded to publish his works at a measured pace, the first to be published was *The Human Phenomenon* in 1955 and the last, the thirteenth, in 1976. He had believed that the Church was in need of another Council like the Council of Nicæa, one that would bring out the cosmic aspect of the God–Man and state the value of the world and human work. A few years after the death of Teilhard, a new pope, John XXIII, called for an ecumenical Council, the Second Vatican Council (1962–65). There the name of Teilhard was mentioned four times in deliberations in the main aula, and many can see his influence in the Council document, 'The Church in the Modern World'. The document speaks of Christ as Omega and the goal of human history. It tells of humanity today being 'struck with wonder at its own discoveries and power'. Noting 'collective strivings,' it asks that individuals and nations join together to become 'artisans of a new humanity'. And notes, 'The future of humanity lies in the hands of those who are strong enough to provide coming generations with reasons for living and hope.'

I first read Teilhard during the Council. I was then in a Jesuit seminary studying for the priesthood. A fellow seminarian kept pressing me to read Teilhard. At the time I had many books that I wanted to read, so I said Yes—not quite meaning it. One morning I returned to my room to find that a copy of *The Divine Milieu* had been placed on my desk. I stood for a moment flipping through the pages till my eye came upon the dedication: '*Sic Deus dilexit mundum*: For those who love the world.'[27] I had read many spiritual books, but they never quite spoke to me; I had too much love for the world. I sat down to further consider the text and found sentence after sentence leaping off the page: 'Greater still, Lord, let your universe be greater still, so that I may hold you and be held by you by a contact at once made ever more intense and ever wider in its extent!'[28] I turned the pages with mounting excitement, for an author was speaking to me as no other author had! I did not understand all that I read, but I proceeded

[27] *The Divine Milieu*, p. ii.
[28] *Ibid.*, p. 3.

through the text at one sitting. I seemed to make a spiritual journey in the process until I came to the passage where the journey ended: 'Now the earth can certainly clasp me in her giant arms. She can swell me with her life, or take me back into her dust . . . But her enchantments can no longer do me any harm, since she has become for me, over and above herself, the body of him who is and of him who is coming.'

Since my first reading of *The Divine Milieu*, I have talked with many who knew Teilhard, I have studied his texts, written much about him, taught courses on his thought, and shared in many large Teilhard conferences. In this I have met many others who find Teilhard speaks to them as he speaks to me. One of these is Siôn Cowell who has done the present translation. We share a common mission: to let the words of Teilhard reach out to others—who love the world.

Shortly before he died, Teilhard looked back on *The Divine Milieu*, and felt he could not speak again with the same freshness and enthusiasm, but he assures us the wonder and the passion remained. In being asked to write a Foreword to this new translation, I have looked over it and find it a fine piece of work. For Siôn Cowell it has been a labor of love. The basic ideas are familiar now, but sentences of the new translation again leap from the page and my wonder and passion remain.

September 2003
Georgetown University

TRANSLATOR'S NOTE

This newly-revised translation seeks to respond to what many have long seen as an urgent need to bring Teilhard's spiritual masterpiece to a world that is foundering, in his own words, not in atheism, but in unsatisfied theism.[1]

'These pages,' Teilhard says in his *Introduction*, 'put forward no more than a practical attitude—or, more exactly perhaps, a way of teaching how to see.' *The Divine Milieu* was written not for those who were comfortable in their Catholic Faith, but for the doubters and the waverers—those for whom classical expressions of religious faith had long lost their meaning. Doubters and waverers there will always be. And the present translation has been made with these individuals in mind.

Teilhard chose the word 'milieu' with great care. He had already used it in the title of his 1917 essay 'The Mystical Milieu.' He uses it here in its particularly French sense of expressing at one and the same time the idea of a centre (with no fixed point) and a sphere (with no fixed circumference).[2] It is directly inspired by S. Paul when he tells the Athenians: 'In him we live and move and have our being' (Acts 17.28).

[1] Cf. Pierre Teilhard de Chardin SJ (1881–1955), 'The Zest for Living' (1950), *Activation of Energy*, London: Collins, 1970, pp. 239–40.

[2] Literally, *mi-lieu*, middle: *Le Petit Robert* et *La Larousse de la langue française* trace the word at least as far back as the twelfth century. Cf. Siôn Cowell, *The Teilhard Lexicon* (Brighton & Portland: Sussex Academic Press, 2001), pp. 116–17 and passim. Teilhard's understanding of the 'divine milieu' is inspired, perhaps, by Pascal who speaks of 'an infinite sphere whose centre is everywhere and whose circumference is nowhere' (Blaise Pascal, 1623–1662, fragment 185, in *Pensées*, Paris: Gallimard, 1977, p. 154).

Modern translators are frequently troubled by the French word 'Homme'. In *The Divine Milieu* it embraces both men and women. However, the singular 'Man' is no longer considered an acceptable translation by those who have not yet found a satisfactory gender-neutral equivalent in modern English. Consequently, I have followed modern practice in opting for the third person plural wherever necessary.

Teilhard's frequent use of Latin words and phrases would have seemed quite normal to his contemporaries—particularly those familiar with the *Vulgate* (the Latin Bible used in the Catholic Church until after the Second Vatican Council, 1962–65). This is, of course, no longer the case. And so, while opting to retain the original Latin in the text, I have provided English translations in the footnotes.

Teilhard began writing *The Divine Milieu* in Tientsin (Tianjin), China, in November 1926. By March 1927 it had already been completed. His superiors in the Society of Jesus forbade publication then and later. They even tried—and failed—to prevent publication after his death in 1955. In his lifetime numerous stenciled copies were made by friends and sympathizers. Indeed, during the Second World War hundreds if not thousands of copies are said to have been passed among French prisoners of war in Germany. And a limited edition of just 30 copies had even been printed in 1938 by the catholic press in Beirut *'ad usum manuscripti'*. Teilhard himself knew nothing of this until he was given a copy on his return to Paris from China in 1946. Over the years he made various changes to the text which were fully taken into account in the 1957 French edition—the text on which this revised English translation is based.

The original English translation by Bernard Wall and others has served us well for nearly half a century. It has long been ripe for revision. But this in itself poses a problem for potential translators. How should one convey the message in contemporary language while remaining faithful as far as possible to Teilhard's original vision? One of Teilhard's biographers, his friend and confrère René d'Ouince, anticipated this question when he wrote: 'Almost certainly his "ideas" and especially his cosmology will, like all cosmologies, become dated.

What will remain is that at a particular moment of history, in a particular cultural milieu, a particular believer had a vision of the undoubted grandeur of the world. After a certain period of decline I believe that the influence of Teilhard will take on a new lease of life. He will be read as we read the great classics...'.[3] Julian Huxley wrote of Teilhard that 'he has given the world a picture not only of rare clarity but pregnant with compelling conclusions'. Teilhard was a man of vision and great energy, which he passed on via his substantial body of writing. As new English-language translations of the Collected Works become available—works that construct a synthesis of mysticism, spirit, science and faith—they will have a renewed affect and influence on our understanding of the place of the human species on planetary and cosmic evolution.

Siôn Cowell
Feast of the Transfiguration
August 6, 2003

---

[3] René d'Ouince SJ (1896–1973), *Un prophète en procès: Teilhard de Chardin et l'avenir de la pensée chrétienne*, Aubier, 1977, II, pp. 266–67.

PREFACE

If the form and content of the following pages are to be rightly understood, readers should not misconceive the spirit in which they were written.

This book is not specifically addressed to christians who are firmly established in their faith and have nothing more to learn about its beliefs. It is written for the waverers, both inside and outside; that is, for those who instead of giving themselves wholly to the Church,* either hesitate on its threshold or turn away in the hope of going beyond it.

As a result of changes which, over the last hundred years or more, have modified our empirically based picture of the world and consequently the moral value of many of its elements, the 'human religious ideal' tends to stress certain trends and to express itself in terms which seem, at first sight, no longer to coincide with the 'christian religious ideal'.

So it is that those whose education or instinct leads them to listen primarily to the voices of the earth, have a certain fear that they may be false to themselves or diminish themselves if they simply follow the Gospel path.

So the purpose of this essay—on life or on interior vision—is to prove by a kind of tangible confirmation that this fear is unfounded, since the most traditional christianity, expressed in Baptism, the

---

* By 'Church' Teilhard usually means the 'Catholic Church' understood as the family of local churches in communion with the Church of Church of Rome and its bishop. This is very much in line with Vatican II ecclesiology.

Cross and the Eucharist, can be interpreted to embrace all that is best in the aspirations peculiar to our times.

May it help to show that Christ, who is ever the same and ever new, has never ceased to be the 'first' within humanity.

An Important Observation

The following pages do not pretend to offer a complete treatise on ascetical theology[†]—they only offer a simple description of a psychological evolution observed over a specified period. A possible series of interior perspectives gradually revealed to the mind in the course of a humble yet 'illuminative' ascent—that is all we have tried to note down here.

Readers should not, therefore, be surprised at the apparently small space allotted to moral evil, to sin: the soul with which we are dealing is assumed to have already turned away from the path of error.

Nor should the fact arouse concern that the action of grace is not referred to or invoked more explicitly. The subject under consideration is the human being, actual, concrete, 'supernaturalized'—seen in the domain of their conscious psychology only. So there was no need to distinguish explicitly between natural and supernatural, between divine influence and human operation. But although these technical terms are absent, the action of grace is everywhere taken for granted. Not only as a theoretically admitted entity, but also as a living reality, the notion of grace impregnates the whole atmosphere of my book.

And in fact the divine milieu would lose all its grandeur and all its savor for 'mystics' if they did not feel, with their whole 'participated' being, with their whole soul made receptive of the divine favor freely poured out upon it, with their whole will strengthened and encouraged, if they did not feel so completely swept away in the divine ocean that no initial point of support would be left them in the end, of their own, within themselves, from which they could act.

[†] 'The systematic consideration of the existential truths and problems of concrete christian life with a view to their mastery by the individual christian' (Karl Rahner and Herbert Vorgrimler, eds., *Dictionary of Theology*, Crossroad, 1981, p. 28).

The Divine Milieu

INTRODUCTION

'In eo vivimus' [1]

The enrichment and ferment of religious thought in our time has undoubtedly been caused by the revelation of the size and unity of the world all around and within us. All around us the physical sciences are endlessly extending the unfathomable depths of time and space, and ceaselessly discerning new connections between the elements of the universe. Within us a whole world of affinities and interrelated sympathies, as old as the human soul, is being awakened by the stimulus of these great discoveries, and what has hitherto been dreamed rather than experienced is at last taking shape and consistency. Scholarly and discriminating among serious thinkers, simple or pedantic among the less well-educated, the aspirations towards a vaster and more organic One,[2] and the premonitions of unknown energies and their application in new fields, are the same and are emerging simultaneously on all sides. It is almost a commonplace today to find men and women who, quite naturally and unaffectedly, live in the explicit consciousness of being an atom or a citizen of the universe.

This collective awakening, similar to what, at some given moment, makes individuals realize the true dimensions of their own lives, must inevitably have a profound religious reaction on the mass of humanity—either to cast down or to exalt.

---

[1] 'In him we live' (Acts 17.28—New King James Version NKJ). Unless otherwise indicated translations are from the New Revised Standard Version (NRSV).
[2] 'Concept representing an act of synthesis of the multiple—primordial dust at the beginning of evolution that supports the process of centration and union—at each stage of evolution' (Siôn Cowell, *The Teilhard Lexicon*, Sussex Academic Press, 2001, pp. 121, 135).

For some, the world has disclosed itself as too vast. Within such immensity, human beings are lost, they no longer count: there is nothing left for them to do but shut their eyes and disappear. For others, on the contrary, the world is too beautiful: it, and it alone, must be adored.

There are christians (as there are men and women) who remain unaffected by these feelings of anxiety or fascination. The following pages are not for them. But there are others who are alarmed by the agitation or the attraction irrepressibly produced in them by this new rising star. Is the Christ of the Gospels, imagined and loved within the dimensions of a Mediterranean world, capable of still embracing and still forming the center of our prodigiously expanding universe? Is the world not in process of becoming more vast, more intimate, more dazzling than Jehovah? Will it not burst our religion asunder? Will it not eclipse our God?

Without yet daring, perhaps, to admit to this anxiety, there are however many (as I know from having come across them all over the world . . .) who feel it deep within themselves. It is for these that I am writing.

I shall not attempt to embark on a metaphysics or an apologetics. But I shall go back, with those who would like to follow me, to the Agora. There, together, we shall listen to S. Paul telling the Areopagites[3] of 'God, who made us that we might seek him—God whom we try to apprehend by the groping of our lives—this God is as pervasive and tangible as the atmosphere in which we are bathed. He encompasses us on all sides, like the world itself. What prevents you, then, from enfolding him in your arms? One thing only: your inability to see him.'[4]

---

[3] Acts 17.22 ff.

[4] 'In the course of my whole life, through my whole life, little by little the world has caught fire, energized to become, all around me, wholly luminous from within . . . Such has been my experience of contact with the earth—the diaphany of the divine at the heart of a universe on fire . . . Christ. His heart. A fire: capable of penetrating everything—and little by little spreading everywhere.' ('Le Christique' (1955), *Le Cœur de la matière*, Seuil, 1976, pp. 21, 22 (our translation); cf. 'The Christic' (1955), *The Heart of Matter*, Collins, 1978, pp. 15, 16). (French Editor's Note.)

2

This little book does no more than recapitulate the eternal lesson of the Church in the words of someone who, because he believes himself to feel deeply in tune with his own times, has tried to teach how to see God everywhere, in all that is most hidden, most solid and most ultimate in the world. These pages put forward no more than a practical attitude—or, more exactly perhaps, a way of teaching how to see.[5] Let us begin by leaving argument aside for a moment. Put yourself where I am and look around you. From this privileged position, which is no hard-won height reserved for the elect but the solid platform built by two thousand years of christian experience, you will see how easily the two stars, whose divergent attractions were disorganizing your faith, are brought into conjunction. Without mixture, without confusion, God, the true christian God, will, before your eyes, invade the universe, our universe of today, a universe which so frightened you by its alarming size or its pagan[6] beauty. He will penetrate it as a ray of light does a crystal; and, with the help of the great layers of creation, he will become for you universally tangible and active—very near and very distant at one and the same time.

If you are able to focus your soul's regard to perceive this magnificence, you will soon forget, I promise, your unfounded fears in face of the mounting significance of the earth; and your one thought will be to exclaim: *'Greater still, Lord, let your universe be greater still, so that I may hold you and be held by you by a contact at once made ever more intense and ever wider in its extent!'*

The line we shall follow in our study is quite simple. Since in the field of experience our existence can properly be divided into two parts—what we do and what we undergo—we shall consider in turn

[5] 'One could say that the whole of life lies in seeing—if not ultimately, at least essentially . . . See or perish. That is the situation imposed on every element of the universe by the mysterious gift of existence. And thus, to a higher degree, this is the human condition' (Pierre Teilhard de Chardin, *The Human Phenomenon*, Sussex Academic Press, 1999, p. 3).
[6] *Pagan*, Lat. *paganus*, peasant, originally one who was not a monotheist but a polytheist: used by Teilhard in the sense of one who is not a christian but is deeply attached to Mother Earth.

our activities and our passivities. In each we shall find at the beginning that, in accordance with his promise, God truly awaits us in things—unless he comes to meet us. Next we shall marvel how the manifestation of his sublime presence in no way disturbs the harmony of our human attitude but, on the contrary, brings it its true form and perfection. This done, that is, having shown that the two halves of our lives (and consequently our whole world) are full of God, it will remain for us to make an inventory of the wonderful properties of this milieu which is all around us (and which is however beyond and underlying everything), the only one in which, from now on, we are equipped to breathe freely.

PART ONE

The Divinization of
Our Activities

Of the two halves or components into which we can divide our lives, the most important, judging by appearances and by the price we set upon it, is the sphere of activity,[7] effort and development. There can, of course, be no action without reaction. And, again, there is nothing in us which in origin and at its deepest is not, as S. Augustine said, *'in nobis sine nobis'* ('in us without us').[8] When we act, it seems, with the greatest spontaneity and vigor, we are to some extent led by the things we imagine we are controlling. Moreover, the very expansion of our energy (which reveals the core of our autonomous personality) is, ultimately, only our obedience to a will to be and to grow of which we can master neither the varying intensity nor the countless modes. We shall return at the beginning of Part Two to these essential passivities, some of which form part of the very marrow of our being, while others are diffused among the interplay of universal causes which we call 'our character', 'our nature' or 'our good and bad luck'. For the moment let us consider our life in terms of the categories and definitions which are the most immediate and most common. We can all distinguish quite clearly between the moments when we are acting and those when we are acted upon. Let us consider ourselves in one of those phases of dominant activity and try to see how, with the help of our activity and by developing it to the full, the divine presses in upon us and seeks to enter our lives.

---

[7] It is especially important at this point to bear in mind what was said in the *Preface*. When we speak of 'activity' we use the word in the ordinary, everyday sense, without in any way denying, far from it, all that occurs between grace and will in the infra-experiential spheres of the soul. To repeat: what is most divine in God is that, in an absolute sense, we are nothing apart from him. The least injection of what may be called pelagianism would suffice to ruin immediately the beauties of the divine milieu in the eyes of the 'seer'. (Author's Note.)

[8] Usually translated as 'God works in us without our action' (S. Augustine of Hippo, 354–430).

1

The undoubted existence of the fact
and the difficulty of explaining it:
The christian problem of the sanctification of action

Nothing is more certain, dogmatically, than the possible sanctification of human action. 'Whatever you do in word or deed,' says S. Paul, 'do all in the name of our Lord Jesus Christ.'[9] And the most cherished of christian traditions has always been to understand 'in the name of our Lord Jesus Christ' in the sense of 'in intimate union with our Lord Jesus Christ'. Is it not S. Paul himself who, after calling on us to 'put on Christ',[10] goes on to forge the famous series of words *'collaborare, compati, commori, con-ressuscitare'*, giving them the fullest possible meaning, a literal meaning even, and expressing the conviction that every human life must, in some way, become a life in common with the life of Christ? The actions of life of which S. Paul is speaking here should not, we know, be understood solely in the sense of works of religion or devotion (prayers, fasting, almsgiving, etc.). It is the whole of human life, down to its most 'natural' zones, which the Church teaches can be sanctified. 'Whether you eat or whether you drink', says S. Paul.[11] The whole history of the Church is there to prove it. Taken as a whole, then, from the most solemn declarations or statements of Popes and Doctors of the Church to the advice humbly given by a priest in the secret of the confessional, the general influence and practice of the Church has always been to dignify, exalt and transfigure in God the duties inherent in our lives, the search for natural truth, and the development of human action.

The fact cannot be denied. But its legitimacy, that is, its logical coherence with the whole basis of the christian spirit, is not immediately evident. How is it that the perspectives opened up by the

---

[9] Cf. Col 3.17 (NRSV, NKJ).
[10] Gal 3.27.
[11] 1 Cor 10.31.

Kingdom of God do not, by their very presence, shatter the distribution and balance of our activities? How can those who believe in heaven and the Cross continue to believe seriously in the value of worldly occupations? How can believers, in the name of everything that is most christian in them, carry out their human duty to the fullest extent and as whole-heartedly and freely as if they were on the direct road to God? This is what is not altogether clear at first sight; and in fact disturbs more minds than we think.

The question might be put in this way:

According to the most sacred articles of their Creed,[12] christians believe that life here below is continued in a life of which the joys, the sufferings, the reality, are quite out of proportion to the present conditions in our universe. This contrast and disproportion are enough, by themselves, to rob us of our taste for the world and our interest in it; but to them must be added a positive doctrine of judgment upon, even disdain for, a fallen and vitiated world. 'Perfection consists in detachment; all that is around us is vanity and ashes.' Believers constantly read or hear these austere words. How can they reconcile them with that other counsel, usually coming from the same master and in any case written in their hearts by nature, that they must be an example to the Gentiles[13] in devotion to duty, in energy, and even in leadership, in all the spheres opened up by human activity? There is no need for us to consider the wayward or the lazy who cannot be bothered to acquire an understanding of their world, or seek with care to advance their fellows' welfare, from which they will benefit a hundredfold after their last breath, and only contribute to the human task 'with the tips of their fingers'. But there is a kind of human spirit (known to every spiritual director)[14] for whom this difficulty assumes the shape and importance of a contin-

---

[12] Cf. the Nicene-Constantinopolitan Creed or Symbol (*Symbolum Nicæno-Constantinopolitanum*).

[13] *Gentile* is used here in the thomist sense of a non-believer.

[14] *Spiritual director*, name given to the person who 'directs' retreatants or exercitants making *The Spiritual Exercises* of S. Ignatius of Loyola (1491–1556), founder and first general of the Society of Jesus (Jesuits).

uing and paralyzing uncertainty. Such spirits, set upon interior unity, become the victims of a veritable spiritual dualism. On the one hand, a very sure instinct, mingled with their love for being and their taste for life, draws them to the joy of creating and knowing. On the other hand, a higher will to love God above all else makes them afraid of the least division or deflection in their affections. In the most spiritual layers of their being they experience a tension between the opposing ebb and flow caused by the drawing power of the two rival stars of which we spoke at the beginning: God and the world. Which of the two is to make itself more nobly adored?

Depending on the more or less vigorous nature of the individuals concerned, this conflict is in danger of ending in one of three ways: either christians will repress their taste for the tangible, force themselves to confine their concerns to purely religious objects, and try to live in a world they have divinized by banishing the largest possible number of earthly objects; or else, harassed by that interior conflict which hampers them, they will dismiss the evangelical counsels and decide to lead what seems to them a complete and human life; or else, again, and this is the most usual case, they will give up trying to make sense of their situation; never belonging wholly to God, nor ever wholly to things; incomplete in their own eyes, and insincere in the eyes of their contemporaries, they will gradually acquiesce in a double life. I am speaking, it should not be forgotten, from experience.

For various reasons, all three solutions are to be feared. Whether we become distorted, disgusted, or divided, the result is equally bad, and certainly contrary to what christianity should rightly produce in us. There is, without possible doubt, a fourth way out of the problem: it consists in seeing how, without making the smallest concession to 'nature' but with a thirst for greater perfection, we can reconcile and provide mutual nourishment for a love of God and a healthy love of the world, a striving towards detachment and a striving towards the enrichment of our human lives.

Let us look at the two solutions, the first incomplete, the second complete, that can be brought to the christian problem of 'the divinization of human effort'.

2

An incomplete solution: human action has no value other than the intention which directs it

If we try somewhat crudely to reduce to its barest bones the immediate answer given by spiritual directors to those who ask them how christians, who are determined to spurn the world and jealously keep their hearts for God, can love what they are doing (in conformity with the Church's teaching that the faithful should play, not a lesser, but a fuller part than the pagan), it will run along these lines:

'You are anxious, my friend, to restore value to your human labor; to you the characteristic viewpoints of christian asceticism seem to set far too little store by such activity. Very well then, you must let the clear spring water of purity of intention flow into your works, as if it were its very substance. Purify your intention, and the least of your actions will be filled with God.

'Certainly the material side of your actions has no definitive value. Whether men or women discover one truth or one fact more or less, whether or not they make beautiful music or beautiful pictures, whether their organization of the world is more or less successful— none of this has any direct importance for heaven. None of these discoveries or creations will constitute one of the stones of which the New Jerusalem is built. But what will count, up there, what will always endure, is this: that you have acted in all things conformably to the will of God.

'God obviously has no need of the products of your busy activity, since he could give himself everything without you. The only thing that concerns him, the only thing he desires intensely, is your faithful use of your freedom, and the preference you accord him over the things around you.

'Try to grasp this: the things which are given to you on earth are given you purely as an exercise, a "blank sheet" on which you make your own mind and heart. You are on a testing-ground where God can judge whether you are capable of being translated to heaven and

11

into his presence. You are on trial. So that it matters very little what becomes of the fruits of the earth or what they are worth. The whole question is whether you have used them to learn how to obey and how to love.

'You should not, therefore, set store by the coarse outer-covering of your human actions. This can be burned like straw or smashed like china. Think, rather, that into each of these humble vessels you can pour, like a sap or a precious liqueur, the spirit of obedience and union with God. If worldly aims have no value in themselves, you can love them for the opportunity they give you of proving your faithfulness to God.'

We would not want to suggest that these words have ever been used literally. But we believe that they convey a nuance which is often discernible in spiritual direction, and we are sure, in any case, that they give a fair idea of what a good number of listeners and exercitants have understood and retained of the exhortations given them.

On this assumption let us examine the attitude they recommend.

In the first place this attitude contains an important element of truth. It is perfectly correct to exalt the role of a good intention as the necessary beginning and foundation of all else; indeed (we shall have to say again) it is the golden key which unlocks our interior personal world to the divine presence. It expresses vigorously the primary worth of the divine will which, by virtue of this attitude, becomes for christians (as for their divine model) the fortifying marrow of all earthly nourishment. It reveals a kind of unique milieu, unchanging beneath the diversity and plurality of human tasks, in which we can place ourselves without ever having to leave.

These various features convey a first and essential approximation to the solution we are looking for; and we shall certainly retain them in their entirety in the more satisfactory plan of the interior life which will soon be suggested. But they seem to us to lack the achievement which our spiritual peace and joy so imperiously demand. The divinization of our effort by the value of the intention put into it, infuses a priceless soul into all our actions; but it does not confer the hope of resurrection upon their bodies. Yet this hope is what we need if our joy is to be complete. It is certainly a very great thing to be able to think that, if we love God, something of our interior activity, of our *operatio*, will never be lost. But will not the very work of our minds, our hearts, and our hands—our achievements, our work, our *opus*—will not this, too, in some way be 'eternalized' and saved?

Indeed, Lord, it will be—by virtue of a claim which you yourself have implanted at the very center of my will! I desire and I need that it should be so.

I desire it because I love irresistibly all that your continuous help enables me to bring each day to reality. A thought, a material improvement, a harmony, a particular nuance of human love, an enchanting complexity of a smile or a glance, all these new beauties that appear for the first time, in me or around me, on the human face of the earth, I cherish them like children and cannot believe that they will die entirely in their flesh. If I believed that these things were to perish for ever, should I have given them life? The more I examine myself, the more I discover this psychological truth: that we shall never lift a finger to do the smallest task unless we are moved, however obscurely, by the conviction that we are contributing infinitesimally (at least indirectly) to the building of something definitive, that is, to your work, my God. This may well sound strange or exaggerated to those who act without thoroughly scrutinizing themselves. And yet it is a fundamental law of their action. It requires no less than the pull of what we call the Absolute— no less than you yourself—to set in motion the frail liberty which you have given us. And that being so, everything which diminishes my explicit faith in the heavenly value of the results of my effort, diminishes irremediably my power to act.

Show all your faithful, Lord, how in a full and true sense 'their work follows them' into your Kingdom: 'opera sequuntur illos' ('They will rest from their labors, for their deeds follow them').[15] *Otherwise they will become like those idle workers who are not spurred by their task. And even if a sound human instinct prevails over the hesitations or the sophisms of an incompletely enlightened religious practice, they will remain fundamentally divided and frustrated; and it will be said that the children of heaven cannot compete on the human level, in conviction and consequently on equal terms, with the children of the world.*

---

[15] Rev 14.13.

13

3

The definitive solution: all effort cooperates to complete the world 'In Christo Iesu'

The general economy of salvation[16] (that is, the divinization) of our work can be expressed briefly as follows:

In our universe, every soul exists for God in our Lord.

But all reality, even material reality, around every one of us, exists for our souls.

Consequently, all sensible reality, around every one of us, exists, through our souls, for God in our Lord.

Let us examine each proposition of the syllogism[17] in succession. The terms and the connecting link are easy to grasp. But we must be careful: it is one thing to have understood the words and another to have penetrated the astonishing world whose inexhaustible riches are revealed by its calm and formal exactitude.

A. *In our universe, every soul exists for God in our Lord*

The major[18] of the syllogism does no more than express the fundamental catholic[19] dogma which all other dogmas merely explain or define. It therefore requires no proof here; but it does need to be strictly understood by the intelligence. Every soul exists for God in our Lord. We should not be content to give this destination of our being in Christ a meaning too obviously modeled on the legal

---

[16] This essentially theological expression is found in the *Catechism of the Catholic Church*, Geoffrey Chapman, 1994, §§ 489, 1092, 1095, 1168.

[17] *Syllogism*, a logically consistent argument consisting of two propositions (major and minor premises), and a conclusion deduced from them.

[18] *Major, major premise*, statement of a general rule forming the first proposition of a syllogism.

[19] Teilhard uses 'catholic' here and elsewhere in the sense of those who are in communion with the Church of Rome and its bishop. This again is in line with Vatican II ecclesiology.

14

relationships which in our world connect an object to its owner. Its nature is altogether more physical and deeper. Because the consummation of the world (what S. Paul calls the Pleroma)[20] is a communion of persons (the Communion of Saints), our minds require that we should express the connections within this communion by analogies drawn from society. Doubtless, to avoid the pantheist[21] and materialist perversion which lies in wait for our thought whenever it applies the powerful but dangerous resources of organic analogies to its mystical concepts, many theologians (more cautious on this point than S. Paul) do not favor too realist an interpretation of the connections which bind the limbs to the head in the Mystical Body. But there is no reason why caution should become timidity. If we want a full and vivid understanding of the teachings of the Church (which alone makes them beautiful and acceptable) on the value of human life and the promises or threats of future life—then, without rejecting anything of the forces of freedom and consciousness which form the natural endowment proper to the human soul, we must perceive the existence of connections between us and the Incarnate Word no less precise than those which control, in the world, the affinities of the elements in the building up of 'natural' wholes.

There is no point, here, in seeking a new name by which to designate the super-eminent nature of this dependence, where all that is

---

[20] 'A rare word of obscure meaning in the NT (Col 1.19; 2.9; Eph 1.23; Jn 1.16) ... S. Paul seems to mean that Jesus Christ is not one of a number of spiritual powers in the world (as gnosticism supposed in "polytheistic fashion"), but that in him the fullness, the one absolute totality, of the divine salvific being is redemptively communicated to us with unequivocal reality ("bodily"), so that we have received from this "fullness" in such abundance as to be "filled", simply speaking. Considered collectively as the Church we are fullness (received) itself, since in this way God is "all in all" (1 Cor 15.28).' (Karl Rahner and Herbert Vorgrimler, eds., *Dictionary of Theology*, p. 389; cf. Siôn Cowell, *The Teilhard Lexicon*, Sussex Academic Press, 2001, pp. 157–8).

[21] Teilhard is a true panentheist (God is in all and all is in God). 'This form of pantheism does not simply identify the world with God in monistic fashion (God, the "All") but sees the "All" of the world "within" God as an interior modification and manifestation of God, although God is not absorbed into the world' (Karl Rahner and Herbert Vorgrimler, eds., *Dictionary of Theology*, p. 359).

most flexible in human combinations and all that is most intransigent in organic structures, merge harmoniously in a moment of final incandescence. We will continue to call it by the name that has always been used: mystical union. Far from implying some idea of diminution, we use the term to mean the strengthening and purification of the reality and urgency contained in the most powerful interconnection revealed to us in every order of the physical and human world. On this path we can advance without fear of over-stepping the truth; for everyone in the Church of God is agreed upon the fact itself, if not upon its systematic statement: by virtue of the powerful Incarnation of the Word, our soul is wholly dedicated to Christ and centered upon him.

B. *'In our universe,' we added, 'in which every spirit exists for God in our Lord, all that is sensible, in its turn, exists for the spirit'*

In the form in which we have given it, the minor[22] of our syllogism is tinged with a certain finalist doctrine which may shock those with a positivist frame of mind. However it does no more than express an incontrovertible natural fact—which is that our spiritual being is continually nourished by the countless energies of the tangible world. Here, again, proof is unnecessary. But it is essential to see—to see things as they are and to see them really and intensely. Unfortunately we live in the network of cosmic influences as we live in the human crowd or among the myriads of stars, without being aware of their immensity. If we wish to live our humanity and our christianity to the full, we must overcome this insensitivity which tends to conceal things from us to the extent that they are too close to us or too vast. Let us, then, perform the salutary exercise which consists in starting with those elements of our conscious life in which our awareness of ourselves as persons is most fully developed, and moving beyond

---

[22] *Minor, minor premise*, 'the premise in a syllogism that contains the minor term or subject of the conclusion'.

these to consider the spread of our being in the world. We shall be astonished at the extent and the intimacy of our relations with the universe.

Where are the roots of our being? In the first place they plunge down into the unfathomable past. How great is the mystery of the first cells which were one day animated by the breath of our souls! What an indecipherable synthesis of successive influences in which we are for ever incorporated! In every one of us, through matter, the whole history of the world is partially reflected. And however autonomous our soul, it is indebted to an inheritance worked upon from all sides—before ever it came into being—by the totality of the energies of the earth: it meets and rejoins life at a determined level. Then, hardly has it entered actively into the universe at this particular point than it feels, in its turn, besieged and penetrated by the flow of cosmic influences which have to be ordered and assimilated. Let us look around us: the waves come from all sides and from the farthest horizon. Through every cleft the world we perceive floods us with its riches—food for the body, nourishment for the eyes, harmony of sounds and fullness of the heart, unknown phenomena and new truths, all these treasures, all these stimuli, all these calls, coming to us from the four corners of the world, cross our consciousness at every moment. What is their role within us? What will their effect be, even if we welcome them passively or indistinctly, like poor workers? They will merge into the most intimate life of our soul and either develop it or poison it. Look at ourselves for one moment and we shall realize this, and either feel delight or anxiety. If even the most humble and most material of our foods is capable of deeply influencing our most spiritual faculties, what can be said of the infinitely more penetrating energies conveyed to us by the music of tones, of notes, of words, of ideas? We do not have a body which takes its nourishment independently of our soul. Everything that the body has admitted and has begun to transform must be transfigured by the soul in its turn. The soul does this, no doubt, in its own way and with its own dignity. But it cannot escape from this universal contact nor from this unremitting labor. And that is how

17

the characteristic power of understanding and loving, which will form its immaterial individuality, is gradually perfected in it for its own good and at its own risk. We hardly know in what proportions and under what guise our natural faculties will pass over into the final act of the divine vision. But it can hardly be doubted that, with God's help, it is here below that we give ourselves the eyes and the heart which a final transfiguration will make the organs of a power of adoration, and of a capacity for beatification, particular to each one us.

The masters of the spiritual life incessantly repeat that God wants only souls. To give those words their true value, we must not forget that the human soul, however independently created our philosophy imagines it to be, is inseparable, in its birth and in its growth, from the universe into which it is born. In every soul, God loves and partly saves the whole world, which this soul sums up in an incommunicable and particular way. But this summing-up, this synthesis, is not given to us ready-made and complete with the first awakening of consciousness. It is we who, through our own activity, must industriously assemble the widely scattered elements. The work of seaweed as it concentrates in its tissues the substances scattered, in infinitesimal quantities, throughout the vast layers of the ocean; the industry of bees as they make honey from the juices dispersed among so many flowers—these are but pale images of the ceaseless working-over that all the forces of the universe undergo in us to become spirit.

Consequently we must all, in the course of our lives, not only show ourselves obedient and docile. But by our fidelity we must build—starting with the most natural territory of our own selves— a work, an *opus*, into which something enters from all the elements of the earth. We make our own soul throughout our earthly lives; and at the same time we collaborate in another work, in another *opus*, which infinitely transcends, while at the same time it narrowly determines, the perspectives of our individual achievement: the completion of the world. Because in presenting the christian doctrine of salvation, it must not be forgotten that the world, taken as a whole,

18

that is, to the extent that it consists in a hierarchy of souls—which appear only successively, develop only collectively and will only be completed in union—the world, too, undergoes a kind of vast 'ontogenesis'[23] in which the development of every soul, assisted by the perceptible realities on which it depends, is but a diminished harmonic. Beneath our efforts to put spiritual form into our own lives, the world slowly accumulates, starting with the whole of matter, what will make of it the Heavenly Jerusalem or the New Earth.

C. *We can now bring together the major and minor of our syllogism to grasp the link between them and the conclusion*

If it is true, as we know from our Creed, that souls enter so intimately into Christ and into God, and if it is true, as we know from the most general conclusions of psychological analysis, that the perceptible enters vitally into the most spiritual zones of our souls—then we must also recognize that in the whole process which from first to last activates and directs the elements of the universe everything forms a single whole. And we begin to see more distinctly rising over our interior world the great sun of Christ the King, of Christ *amictus mundo*, of the Universal Christ.[24] Little by little, stage by stage, everything is finally linked to the supreme center *'in quo omnia constant'* ('in whom all things hold together').[25] The streams which flow from this center operate not only within the higher reaches of the world where human activities take place in a distinctively supernatural and meritorious form. To save and establish these sublime energies, the power of the Word Incarnate penetrates matter itself; it goes down into the deepest depths of the lower forces. And the Incarnation will only be complete when the part of chosen substance contained in

---

[23] *Ontogenesis*, development of an organism.

[24] The 'Universal Christ' and the 'Cosmic Christ' are synonymous in Teilhard's vocabulary (Siôn Cowell, *The Teilhard Lexicon*, pp. 27–8, 30).

[25] Cf. Col 1.17.

every object—given spiritualized once in our souls and a second time with our souls in Jesus—shall have rejoined the final center of its completion. *'Quid est quod ascendit, nisi quod prius descendit, ut repleret omnia?'* ('What is he who ascended to heaven but he who first descended to the lower parts of the earth that he might fill all things?')[26]

It is through the collaboration which he stimulates in us that Christ, starting from all created things, is consummated and attains his plentitude. S. Paul himself tells us so. We may, perhaps, imagine that the creation was finished long ago. But this would be quite wrong. It continues still more magnificently, and at the highest levels of the world. *'Omnis creatura adhuc ingemiscit et parturit'* ('The whole creation has been groaning in labor pains until now').[27] And we serve to complete it, even by the humblest work of our hands. This is, ultimately, the meaning and value of our acts. By virtue of the interrelation between matter, soul and Christ, we bring part of the being which he desires back to God in whatever we do. With each one of our works, we labor, separately, but no less really, to build the Pleroma; that is, we bring to Christ a little completion.

4

Communion through action

Every one of our works, by its more or less remote or direct effect upon the spiritual world, helps to perfect Christ in his mystical totality. This is the fullest possible answer to the question: How can we, following the call of S. Paul, see God in all the active half of our lives? In fact, through the unceasing operation of the Incarnation,

---

[26] Quotation based on S. Paul's words in Eph 4.9–10: *'quod autem ascendit quid est nisi quia et descendit primum in inferiores partes terræ qui descendit ipse est et qui ascendit super omnes cælos ut impleret omnia'* ['When it says, "He ascended," what does it mean but that he had also descended into the lower parts of the earth? He who descended is the same one who ascended far above all the heavens, so that he might fill all things'].

[27] The Vulgate reads: *'omnis creatura ingemescit et parturit usque adhuc'* (Rom 8.22).

the divine so thoroughly penetrates all our creaturely energies that, to meet it and lay hold on it, we could not find a more fitting setting than that of our action.

In action, first of all, I adhere to the creative power of God; I coincide with it; I become not only its instrument but its living extension. And as there is nothing more personal in beings than their will, I merge myself, in a sense, through my heart, with the very heart of God. This contact is continuous because I am always acting; and at the same time, since I can never set a boundary to the perfection of my fidelity nor to the fervor of my intention, this contact enables me to assimilate myself, ever more strictly and indefinitely, to God.

The soul does not pause to relish this communion, nor does it lose sight of the material end of its action; for it is wedded to a creative effort. The will to succeed, a certain passionate delight in the work to be done, form an integral part of our creaturely fidelity. It follows that the very sincerity with which we desire and pursue success for God's sake reveals itself as a new factor—also without limits—in the most perfect conjunction with the All-Powerful who animates us. Originally we had fellowship with God in the simple common exercise of wills; but now we unite ourselves with him in the shared love of the end for which we are working; and the crowning marvel is that, with the possession of this end, we have the utter joy of discovering his presence once again.

All this results directly from what was said a moment ago on the interrelation between natural and supernatural actions in the world. Any increase that I can bring upon myself or upon things is translated into some increase in my power to love and some progress in Christ's blessed hold upon the universe. Our work appears to us, above all, as a way of earning our daily bread. But its essential virtue is on a higher plane: through it we complete in ourselves the subject of the divine union; and through it again we somehow make to grow in stature the divine term of the One with whom we are united, our Lord Jesus Christ. Consequently, whatever our human role may be, whether we are artists, workers or scholars, we can, if we are christians, speed towards the object of our work as though towards an opening on to the supreme fulfillment of our beings. Indeed, without exaggeration or excess in thought or word—but simply by confronting the most fundamental truths of our faith and of experience—we are led to the following observation: God is inexhaustibly attainable in the totality of our action. And this prodigy of divinization has nothing with which we dare to compare it except the subtle, gentle sweetness with which this actual change of shape is wrought; for it is achieved without disturbing at all— *'non minuit, sed sacravit'* ('it is not diminished but consecrated')—the completeness and unity of human effort.

5
Christian perfection of human effort

There was reason to fear, as we have said, that the introduction of christian perspectives might seriously upset the ordering of human action; that the seeking after, and waiting for, the Kingdom of Heaven might deflect human activity from its natural tasks, or at least eclipse any interest entirely in them. Now we see why this cannot and must not be so. The conjunction of God and the world has just taken place under our eyes in the domain of action. No, God does not deflect our gaze prematurely from the work he himself has given us, since he presents himself to us as attainable through this very work. Nor does he blot out, in his intense light, the detail of our earthly aims, since the closeness of our union with him is in fact determined by the exact fulfillment of the least of our tasks. Let us accustom ourselves to this basic truth until we are steeped in it, until it becomes as familiar to us as the perception of shape or the reading of words. God, in all that is most living and incarnate in him, is not distanced from us, altogether apart from the world we see, touch, hear, smell and taste around us. Rather he awaits us every instant in our action, in the work of the moment. There is a sense in which he is at the tip of my pen, my spade, my brush, my needle—of my heart and of my mind. By pressing the stroke, the line, or the stitch, on which I am engaged, to its ultimate natural finish, I shall lay hold of this last end towards which my most interior will tends. Like those formidable physical energies which we succeed in disciplining in order to make them perform operations of prodigious delicacy, so the tremendous power of the divine attraction is focused on our frail desires and microscopic intents without breaking their point. It super-animates; therefore it neither disturbs anything nor stifles anything. It super-animates; therefore it introduces a higher principle of unity into our spiritual life, of which the specific effect is—depending on the point of view we adopt—either to sanctify human effort or to humanize christian life.

A. *Sanctification of human effort*

I do not think I am exaggerating when I say that nine out of ten practicing christians feel that human work is always at the level of a 'spiritual encumbrance'. In spite of the practice of right intentions, and the day offered every morning to God, the general mass of the faithful dimly feel that time spent in the office or in the studio, in the fields or in the factory, is time spent away from prayer and adoration. It is impossible not to work—that is taken for granted. But it is also impossible to aim at the deep religious life reserved for those who have the leisure to pray or preach all day long. A few moments of the day can be salvaged for God, yes, but the best hours are absorbed, or at any rate cheapened, by material cares. Under the sway of this feeling, large numbers of catholics lead a double or crippled life in practice: they have to step out of their human dress to have faith in themselves as christians—and inferior christians at that.

What has been said above of the divine extensions and divine demands of the Mystical or Universal Christ, should be enough to demonstrate both the emptiness of these impressions and the validity of the thesis, so dear to christianity, of sanctification through fulfilling the duties of our station. There are, of course, certain noble and cherished moments of the day—those when we pray or

23

receive the sacraments. If it were not for these moments of more efficient or explicit communication with God, the tide of the divine omnipresence, and our perception of it, would weaken until all that was best in our human effort, without being entirely lost to the world, would for us be emptied of God. But once we have jealously safeguarded our relation to God encountered, if I may dare use the expression, 'in his pure state' (that is, in a state of being distinct from all the constituents of the world), there is no need to fear that the most trivial or the most absorbing of occupations should force us to depart from him. To repeat: by virtue of the Creation and, still more, of the Incarnation, nothing here below is profane to those who know how to see. On the contrary, everything is sacred to those who can distinguish this portion of chosen being which is subject to Christ's drawing power in process of consummation. Try, with God's help, to see the connection—even physical and natural—which ties your labor to the building of the Kingdom of Heaven; try to realize that heaven itself smiles upon you and, through your work, draws you to itself; then, as you leave church for the noisy streets, you will remain with only one feeling, that of continuing to immerse yourself in God. If your work is dull or exhausting, take refuge in the inexhaustible and becalming interest of progressing in the divine life. If your work makes you passionate, let the spiritual impulse which matter communicates to you to enter into your zest for God whom you know better and desire more under the veil of his works. Never, at any time, 'whether eating or drinking', consent to do anything without first of all realizing its significance and constructive value *in Christo Iesu*,[28] and pursuing it with all your might. This is not simply a commonplace precept for salvation: it is the very path to sanctity for every one of us according to our state and calling. For what is sanctity in creatures if not to adhere to God with the maximum of their strength?—and what does this maximum adherence to God mean if not the fulfillment, in the world organized around Christ, of the exact function,

[28] Rom 3.24.

24

be it lowly or eminent, to which those creatures are destined both by natural endowment and by supernatural gift?

We see in the Church all kinds of groups whose members are vowed to the perfect practice of this or that particular virtue: mercy, detachment, splendor of the liturgy, missions, contemplation. Why should there not be men and women vowed to the task of exemplifying, by their lives, the general sanctification of human effort?—people whose common religious ideal would be to give a full and conscious explanation of the divine possibilities or demands which any worldly occupation implies—people, in a word, who would devote themselves, in the fields of thought, art, industry, commerce and politics, etc., to carrying out in the sublime spirit these demands, the basic tasks which form the very bones of human society? Around us the 'natural' progress which nourishes the sanctity of each new century is all too often left to the children of the world, that is, to agnostics or irreligious. Unconsciously or involuntarily such people collaborate in the Kingdom of God and in the fulfillment of the elect: their efforts, going beyond or correcting their incomplete or bad intentions, are gathered in by the one 'whose power subjects all things to itself'.[29] But that is no more than a second best, a temporary phase in the organization of human activity. Right from the hands that knead the dough, to those who consecrate it, the great and universal Host should be prepared and handled in a spirit of adoration.

May the time come when men and women, having been awakened to a sense of the close bond linking all the movements of this world in the single work of the Incarnation, will be unable to give themselves to any of their tasks without illuminating it with the clear vision that their work, however elementary it may be, is received and used by a divine Center of the universe!

When that comes to pass, there will be little to separate life in the cloister from life in the world. And only then will the action of the children of heaven (at the same time as the action of the children of the world) have attained the intended plenitude of its humanity.

---

[29] Cf. '. . . the power that enables him to make all things subject to himself' (Phil 3.21).

B. *Humanization of christian effort*

The great objection brought against christianity in our time, and the real source of the distrust which renders entire blocks of humanity immune to the influence of the Church, has nothing to do with historical or theological difficulties. It is the suspicion that our religion makes its followers inhuman.

'Christianity', the best of the Gentiles sometimes think, 'is bad or inferior because it does not lead its followers to levels of attainment beyond ordinary human powers; rather it withdraws them from the ordinary ways of humanity and sets them on other paths. It isolates them instead of merging them with the mass. It causes them to lose interest in the common task instead of harnessing them to it. Consequently, far from raising them to a higher level, it diminishes them and makes them false to their nature. Moreover, do they not admit as much themselves? And if their religious,[30] or their priests, should happen to devote their lives to research in one of the so-called secular disciplines, they are usually very careful to point out that they are only lending themselves temporarily to serve a passing whim of scholarly fashion or even something ultimately of the stuff of illusion, and that simply to show that christians are not the stupidest of people. When catholics work with us, we invariably get the impression that they are doing so in a spirit of condescension. They appear to be interested, but in fact, because of their religion, they simply do not believe in human effort as such. Their hearts are not really with us. Christianity nourishes deserters and false friends: and this is what we cannot forgive.'

We have put this objection, which would be deadly if it were true, in the mouth of an unbeliever. But has it no echo, here and there, within the most faithful souls? Which christians who have become aware of a sheet of glass insulating them from their non-believing colleagues, have not asked themselves uneasily whether they were not on a false track or had not actually lost touch with the main

---

[30] Members of religious orders or congregations.

current of humanity? Without denying that some christians (by their words more than their deeds) do give grounds for the reproach of being, if not the 'enemies', at least the 'stragglers' of the human race, we can safely assert, after what we said above about the supernatural value of our work on earth, that their attitude is due to an incomplete understanding and not at all to some ineradicable flaw in our religion.

How could we be deserters? How could we be skeptical about the future of the tangible world? How could we be repelled by human labor? How little you know us! You suspect us of not sharing your concerns, your hopes and your excitement as you penetrate the mysteries and conquer the forces of nature. 'Feelings of this kind', you say, 'can only be shared by men and women struggling side by side for existence; whereas you christians profess to be saved already.' As though for us as for you, indeed far more than for you, it were not a matter of life and death that the earth should flourish to the uttermost of its natural powers. As far as you are concerned (and it is here that you are not yet human enough, you do not go to the limits of your humanity) it is simply a matter of the success or failure of a reality which remains vague and precarious even when conceived in the form of some super-humanity. For us it is a question in a true sense of achieving the victory of no less than a God. One thing is infinitely disappointing, I grant you: far too many christians are insufficiently conscious of the 'divine' responsibilities of their lives and live like other men and women, giving only half of themselves, never experiencing the spur of the intoxication of advancing the Kingdom of God in every domain of humanity. But do not blame anything but our weakness: our faith imposes on us the right and the duty to throw ourselves into the things of the earth. As much as you, and even better than you (because, of the two of us, I alone am in a position to prolong the perspectives of my effort to infinity, in conformity with the requirements of my present intention), I want to dedicate myself body and soul to the sacred duty of research. We must test every barrier, try every path, plumb every depth. *'Nihil intentatum . . .'* ('Leave nothing untried . . .'). God wills it, God willed that he should have need of it. You are human, you say? *'Plus et ego'* ('I am a better one').[31]

'Plus et ego'. There can be no doubt of it. At a time when the consciousness of its own powers and possibilities is legitimately awakening in a humanity now ready to become adult, one of the first duties of christians as apologists is to show, by the logic of their religious views and still more by the logic of their action, that the Incarnate God did not come to diminish in us the glorious responsibility and splendid ambition that is ours: of fashioning our own self. Once again, *'non minuit, sed sacravit'* ('It is not diminished but consecrated'). No, christianity is not, as it is sometimes presented and sometimes practiced, an additional burden of observances and obligations to weigh down and increase the already heavy load, or to multiply the already paralyzing ties of our life in society. It is, in fact, an immensely powerful soul which bestows significance and beauty and a new lightness on what we are already doing. It is true that it sets us on the road towards unsuspected heights. But the slope which leads to these heights is linked so closely with the one we were already climbing naturally that there is nothing so distinctively human in christians (and this is what remains to be considered) as their detachment.

6
Detachment through action

There hardly seems room for any dispute between christians about what we have so far said about the intrinsic divinization of human effort, since we have restricted ourselves, in establishing it, to taking, in their correct sense, certain universally recognized theoretical and practical truths and confronting them with each other.

Some readers, however, though without finding any specific flaw in our argument, may feel vaguely upset or uneasy in the face of a

---

[31] Cf. 2 Cor 11.23.

christian ideal which lays such stress on the preoccupations of human development and the pursuit of earthly improvements. They should bear in mind that we are still only half-way along the road which leads to the mountain of the Transfiguration. Up to this point we have only been dealing with the active part of our lives. A little later, when we come to the chapter on passivities and diminishment, the arms of the Cross will begin to dominate the scene more widely. Let us consider it for a moment. In the very optimistic and very broadening attitude which has been roughly outlined above, a true and deep renunciation lies concealed. Those who devote themselves to human duty according to the christian formula, though outwardly they may seem to be immersed in the concerns of the earth, are in fact, down to the very depths of their being, people of great detachment.

In itself work is a manifold instrument of detachment, provided we give ourselves to it faithfully and without rebellion. In the first place it implies effort and victory over inertia. And then, however interesting and spiritual it may be (and the more spiritual it is, the truer this becomes), work is always accompanied by the painful pangs of birth. We can only escape the terrible boredom of monotonous and commonplace duty to find ourselves a prey to the interior tension and anxieties of 'creation'. To create, or organize, material energy, truth or beauty, brings with it an interior torment which prevents those who face its hazards from sinking into the quiet and closed-in life in which grows the vice of egoism and attachment (in the technical sense). Honest workers not only surrender their calm and peace once and for all, but must learn continually to jettison the form which their labor or art or thought first took, and go in search of new forms. To pause, to bask in or possess results, would be a betrayal of action. Again and again they must go beyond themselves, tear themselves away from themselves, leaving behind them their most cherished beginnings. And on that road, which is not so different from the royal road of the Cross as might appear at first sight, detachment does not only consist in continually replacing one object with another of the same order—as kilometers replace kilometers on a flat road. By virtue of a marvelous mounting force contained in things (and which will be analyzed in greater detail when we consider the 'spiritual power of matter'), each reality attained and left behind gives us access to the discovery and pursuit of an ideal of higher spiritual content. Those who spread their sails in the right way to the winds of the earth will always find themselves borne by a current towards the open seas. The more nobly they desire and act, the more avid they become for great and sublime aims to pursue. They will no longer be content with family, country and the remunerative aspect of their work. They will want wider organizations to create, new paths to blaze, causes to uphold, truths to discover, ideals to cherish and defend. So, gradually, the workers no longer belong to themselves. Little by little the great breath of the universe has insinuated itself into them through the fissure of their humble but faithful action, has broadened them, raised them up, borne them on.

It is in christians, provided they know how to make the most of the resources of their faith, that these effects will reach their climax and their crown. As we have seen: from the point of view of the reality, accuracy and splendor of the ultimate end towards which we must aim in the least of our acts, we disciples of Christ are the most favored of men and women. Christians know that their function is to divinize the world in Jesus Christ. In them, therefore, the natural process which drives human action from ideal to ideal and towards objects ever more consistent and universal, reaches, thanks to the support of Revelation, its fullest expansion. And in them, consequently, detachment through action should produce its maximum effectiveness.

And this is perfectly true. Christians as we have described them in these pages, are at once the most attached and the most detached of human beings. Convinced in a way in which the 'worldly' cannot be of the unfathomable importance and value concealed beneath the humblest worldly successes, christians are at the same time as convinced as the hermit of the worthlessness of any success which is envisaged only as an individual benefit (or even a general one) without reference to God. It is God and God alone whom they pursue through the reality of created things. For them, interest lies truly in things, but in absolute dependence upon God's presence in them. The light of heaven becomes perceptible and attainable to them in the crystalline transparency of beings. But they want only this light, and if the light is extinguished, because the object is out of place, or has outlived its function, or has moved itself, then even the most precious substance is only ashes in their sight. Similarly, within themselves and their most personal development, it is not themselves that they are seeking, but what is greater than they, to which they know that they are destined. In their own view they no longer count, no longer exist; they have forgotten and lost themselves in the very effort which is making them perfect. It is no longer the atom which lives, but the universe within it.

Not only have they encountered God in the whole field of tangible activities, but in the course of this first phase of their spiritual development, the divine milieu which has been discovered absorbs their powers in the very proportion in which these laboriously overcome their individuality.

PART TWO

---

*The Divinization of
Our Passivities*

While men and women by the very development of their powers are led to discover ever vaster and higher aims for their actions, they also tend to be dominated by the object of their conquests and, like Jacob wrestling with the Angel, they end by adoring what they were struggling against. The scale of what they have unveiled and unleashed brings them into subjection. And then, because of their nature as element, they are brought to recognize that, in the final act that is to unite them to the All, the two terms of the union are utterly disproportionate. They, the lesser, have to receive rather than to give. They find themselves in the grip of what they thought they could grasp.

Christians, who by right are the first and most human of men and women, are more subject than others to this psychological reversal by which, in the case of all intelligent creatures, joy in action imperceptibly melts into desire for submission, and the exaltation of becoming their own selves into zeal to die in another. Having been perhaps primarily alive to the attractions of union with God through action, they begin to conceive and then to desire a complementary aspect, an ulterior phase, in their communion: one in which they would not develop themselves so much as lose themselves in God.

They do not have to look far to discover possibilities and opportunities for fulfillment in this gift of self. They are offered them at every moment—indeed they besiege them on all sides in the length and depth of the countless servitudes which make us servants far more than masters of the universe.

The moment has come to examine the number, the nature and the possible divinization of our passivities.

1

Extent, depth and diverse forms of human passivities

The passivities of our lives, as we said at the beginning of this study, form half of human existence. This expression means, quite simply, that what is not done by us is, by definition, undergone by us. But this does not in any way prejudge the proportions in which action and passion possess our interior domain. In fact, these two parts of our lives, the active and the passive, are extraordinarily unequal. From our point of view, the active occupies first place because we prefer it and because it is more easily perceived. But in the reality of things the passive is immeasurably the wider and the deeper part.

In the first place the passivities ceaselessly accompany our conscious acts in the form of reactions which direct, sustain or oppose our efforts. On this ground alone they inevitably and precisely coincide with the scope of our activities. But their sphere of influence extends far beyond these narrow limits. If we consider the matter carefully we, in fact, perceive with a kind of dismay that it is only the fine-point of ourselves that comes up into the light of self-consciousness and freedom. We know ourselves and set our own course but within an incredibly small radius of light. Immediately beyond lies impenetrable darkness, though it is full of presences—the night of everything that is within us and around us, without us and in spite of us. In this darkness, as vast, rich, troubled and complex as the past and the present of the universe, we are not inert; we react, because we undergo. But this reaction, which operates outside of our control by an unknown prolongation of our being, is, humanly speaking, still part of our passivities. In fact, everything beyond a certain distance is dark, and yet everything is full of being around us. This is the darkness, heavy with promises and threats, which christians will have to illuminate and animate with the divine presence.

In the midst of the confused energies which people this restless night, our mere presence immediately brings about the formation of two groups which press in upon us and demand to be treated in very different ways. On one side, the friendly and favorable energies, those which support our effort and point the way to success: these are the 'passivities of growth'. On the other, the hostile powers which laboriously obstruct our tendencies, hamper or deflect our progress towards greater-being, and thwart our real or apparent capacities for development: these are the 'passivities of diminishment'.

Let us look at each group in turn; let us look them in the face until, in the depth of their alluring, inexpressive or hostile gaze, we discern the kindling light of the blessed countenance of God.

2
Passivities of growth and the two hands of God

Growth seems so natural to us that we are not used to separating from our action the energies which nourish this action, nor the circumstances which favor its success. And yet *'quid habes quod non accepisti?'* ('What do you have that you did not receive?')[32] We undergo life as much as we undergo death, if not more.

Let us penetrate our most secret selves. Let us examine our being from all sides. Let us try, patiently, to perceive the ocean of forces to which we are subjected and in which our growth is, as it were, steeped. This is a salutary exercise: the depth and universality of our dependence go to make up the embracing intimacy of our communion.

… And so perhaps, for the first time in my life (and I am supposed to meditate every day!), I took the lamp and, leaving the zone of everyday occupations and relationships where everything seems clear, I went down into my innermost self, to the deep abyss from which I feel dimly that my power of action emanates. But as I moved further and further away from the conventional certainties by which social life is superficially illuminated, I became aware that I was losing

---

[32] Cf. 1 Cor 4.7.

37

contact with myself. At each step of the descent a new person was disclosed within me of whose name I was no longer sure, and who no longer obeyed me. And when I had to stop my exploration because the path faded from beneath my steps, I found a bottomless abyss at my feet, and out of it came, arising I know not from where, the current I dare to call my life.

What science will ever be able to reveal to us the origin, nature and character of this conscious power to will and to love which constitutes our life? It is certainly not our effort, nor the effort of anyone around us, which sets this current in motion. And it is certainly not our anxious care, nor that of any of our friends, which prevents its ebb or controls its turbulence. We can, of course, trace back through generations some of the antecedents of the torrent which bears us along; and we can, by means of certain moral and physical disciplines and stimulants, regularize or enlarge the aperture through which the torrent is released into us. But neither that geography nor those artifices help us in theory or in practice to harness the sources of life. My self is given to me far more than it is formed by me. We cannot, Scripture says, add a single hour to our span of life.[33] Still less can we add a unit to the potential of our love, or accelerate by another unit the fundamental rhythm which regulates the ripening of our minds and hearts. In the last resort, the profound life, the fontal life, the new-born life, escape our grasp entirely.

Stirred by my discovery, I then wanted to return to the light of day and forget the disturbing enigma in the comfortable surroundings of familiar things—to begin living again on the surface without imprudently plumbing the depths of the abyss. But then, beneath this very spectacle of the turmoil of life, there reappeared, before my newly-opened eyes, the unknown from which I wanted to escape. This time it was not hiding at the bottom of an abyss; it hid itself in the innumerable strands which form the web of chance, the very stuff of which the universe and my own small individuality are woven. Yet it was the same mystery without a doubt: I recognized

---

[33] Or 'add one cubit to our life' (cf. Mt 6.27).

it. Our mind is disturbed when we try to plumb the depths of the world beneath us. But it reels still more when we try to number the favorable chances which must coincide at every moment if the least of living things is to survive and to succeed in its tasks. After the consciousness of being something other and something greater than myself—a second thing made me dizzy: the supreme improbability, the tremendous unlikelihood of finding myself existing in the heart of a world that has succeeded in being a world.

At this moment, as anyone else will find who cares to make this same interior experience, I felt the distress characteristic of an atom adrift in the universe—the distress which makes human wills founder daily under the crushing number of living things and of stars. And if something saved me, it was hearing the voice of the Gospels, guaranteed by divine successes, saying to me from the depth of the night: *'Ego sum nolite timere'* ('It is I, be not afraid').[34]

Yes, O God, I believe it: and I believe it all the more willingly because it is not only a question of my being consoled but of my being completed: it is you who are at the origin of my impulse and at the end of that continuing pull which throughout my life I can do no other than follow or favor the first impulse and its developments. And it is you who vivify, for me, with your omnipresence (even more than my spirit vivifies the matter which it animates), the myriad influences of which I am the constant object. In the life which wells up in me and in the matter which sustains me, I find much more than your gifts: it is you yourself whom I find, you who makes me participate in your being, you who molds me. Truly in the ruling and in the first disciplining of my living strength, in the continually beneficent play of secondary causes, I touch, as near as possible, the two faces of your creative action; and I encounter and kiss your two marvelous hands: the one which holds us so firmly that it is merged, in us, with the sources of life, and the other whose embrace is so wide that, at its slightest pressure, all the springs of the universe respond harmoniously together. In themselves, these blessed passivities which are for me the will to be, the wish to be thus and thus, and the chance of fulfilling myself according to my desire, are all charged with your influence—an influence which will shortly appear more distinctly to me as the organizing energy

---

[34] Mt 14.27; Mk 6.50; Jn 6.20.

of the Mystical Body. To communicate with you in them in a fontal communion (a communion in the sources of life), I have only to recognize you in them, and to ask you to be ever more present in them.

O God, whose call precedes the very first of our movements, grant me the desire to desire being—that, by means of that divine thirst which is your gift, the access to the great waters may open wide within me. Do not deprive me of the sacred taste for being, that primordial energy, that very first of our points of rest: 'Spiritu principali confirma me' (*'Sustain in me a willing spirit'*).[35] *And you whose loving wisdom forms me out of all the forces and all the hazards of the earth, grant that I may begin to draw in the outline a gesture whose full power will only be revealed to me in the presence of the forces of diminishment and death; grant that, after having desired, I may believe, and believe ardently and, above all things, in your active presence.*

Thanks to you, that expectation and that faith are already full of operative virtue. But how am I to set about showing you, and proving to myself, through some external effort, that I am not one of those who say 'Lord, Lord!' with their lips only? I shall work together with your preventive action, and shall do so doubly. First, to your deep inspiration which commands me to be, I shall respond by taking great care never to stifle nor distort nor waste my power to love and to do. Next, to your all-embracing providence which shows me at each moment, by the events of the day, the next step to take and the next rung to climb, I shall respond by my care never to miss an opportunity of rising 'towards spirit'.

The life of each one of us is, as it were, woven of those two threads: the thread of interior development, through which our ideas and affections and our human and religious attitudes are gradually formed; and the thread of exterior success by which we always find ourselves at the exact point where the whole sum of the energies of the universe meet together to bring about in us the effect which God desires.

O God, may you find me at all times as you desire me and where you would have me be, may you lay hold on me fully—both by the within and the without of myself—so that I may never break this double thread of my life.

---

[35] Ps 50.14 (Vulgate). Ps 50.14 in the Vulgate is Ps 51.12 in modern translations. Pss 9 and 10 were originally one poem (as they are in the Greek and Vulgate). Modern translations separate them after v. 20.

40

3
Passivities of diminishment[36]

To adhere to God hidden beneath the interior and exterior energies which animate our being and sustain it in its development, is ultimately to open ourselves to, and put our trust in, all the breaths of life. We answer to, and 'communicate' with, the passivities of growth by our fidelity in action. Consequently by our very desire to experience God passively we find ourselves brought back to the lovable duty of growth.

The moment has come to plumb the decidedly negative side of our existence—the side on which, no matter how far we search, we cannot discern any happy result or any solid conclusion to what happens to us. It is easy enough to understand that God can be grasped in and through every life. But can God also be found in and through every death? This is what perplexes us deeply. And yet this is what we must learn to acknowledge as a matter of settled habit and practice, unless we abandon all that is most characteristically christian in the christian outlook; and unless we are prepared to forfeit communication with God in one of the most widespread and, at the same time, most profoundly passive and receptive experiences of human life.

The forces of diminishment are our real passivities. Their number is vast, their form infinitely varied, their influence constant. To clarify our ideas and direct our meditation we shall divide them into two groups corresponding to the two forms under which we considered

---

[36] If, in speaking of evil in this section, we do not speak more explicitly of sin, it is because the aim of the following pages being solely to show how all things can help believers to unite themselves to God, there is no need to concern ourselves directly with bad action, that is, with positive gestures of disunion. Sin only interests us here to the extent that it is a weakening, a deviation caused by our personal faults (even when repented), or the pain and the scandal which the faults of others inflict on us. From this point of view it makes us suffer and can be transformed in the same way as any other suffering. That is why physical evil and moral evil are presented here, almost without distinction, in the same chapter on the passivities of diminishment. (Author's Note.)

the forces of growth: the diminishments whose origin lies within us, and the diminishments whose origin lies outside of us.

The external passivities of diminishment are all misfortunes. We have only to look back on our lives to see them springing up on all sides: the barrier which blocks our way, the wall which hems us in, the stone which causes us to deviate from our path, the obstacle which breaks us, the microbe which kills the body, the little word which infects the mind, all the incidents and accidents of varying importance and varying kinds, the tragic interferences (upsets, shocks, severances, deaths) which come between the world of 'other' things and the world that radiates from us. And yet when hail, fire and thieves had taken from Job all his wealth and all his family, Satan could say to God: 'Skin for skin! All that people have they will give to save their lives. But stretch out your hand now and touch his bone and his flesh, and he will curse you to your face.'[37] In a sense the loss of things means little to us because we can always imagine getting them back. What is terrible for us is to be irretrievably cut off from things through some interior and irreversible diminishment.

Humanly speaking, the internal passivities of diminishment form the darkest element and the most despairingly useless years of our lives. Some were waiting to pounce on us when we first awoke: natural failings, physical defects, intellectual or moral weaknesses, as a result of which the field of our activities, of our enjoyment, of our vision, has been pitilessly limited since birth. Others were lying in wait for us later on and appeared as suddenly and brutally as an accident, or as stealthily as an illness. All of us one day or another will come to realize, if we have not done so already, that one or other of these sources of disintegration has lodged itself in the very heart of our lives. Sometimes it is the cells of the body that rebel or become diseased; at other times the very elements of our personality seem to be in conflict or to detach themselves from any kind of order. And then we impotently stand by and watch collapse, rebellion, and inte-

---

[37] Job 2.4–5.

rior tyranny, and no friendly influence can come to our help. And if by chance we escape, to a greater or lesser extent, the critical forms of these assaults which come from deep within us and irresistibly destroy the strength, the light, and the love by which we live, there still remains that slow, essential deterioration which we cannot escape: old age little by little robbing us of ourselves and pushing us on towards the end. Time which postpones possession, time which tears us away from enjoyment, time which condemns us all to death—what a formidable passivity is the passage of time . . .

In death, as in an ocean, all our slow or swift diminishments flow out and merge. Death is the sum and the consummation of all our diminishments: it is evil itself—a purely physical evil, to the extent that it results organically in the material plurality in which we are immersed—but also a moral evil, to the extent that in the society to which we belong, or in ourselves, the wrong use of our freedom, by spreading disorder, converts this manifold complexity of our nature into the source of all evil and all corruption.

Let us overcome death by finding God in it. And, by the same token, the divine will be found in our innermost hearts, in the last stronghold which might have seemed capable of escaping its reach.

Here again, as in the case of the 'divinization' of our human activities, we shall find the christian faith absolutely explicit in its claims and in its practice. Christ has conquered death, not only by suppressing its evil effects, but by reversing its sting. By virtue of his resurrection, nothing inevitably kills any longer, but everything is capable of becoming the blessed touch of the divine hands, the blessed influence of the will of God on our lives. No matter how marred by our faults, or how desperate in its circumstances, our position may be, we can, by a complete re-ordering, correct the world around us, and resume our lives in a favorable sense. *'Diligentibus Deum omnia convertuntur in bonum'* ('All things work together for good for those who love God').[38] That is the fact which dominates all explanation and all discussion.

---

[38] The Vulgate reads: *'diligentibus Deum omnia* cooperantur *in bonum'* (Rom 8.28).

But here again, as in the matter of the saving value of human effort, our minds want to justify to themselves their hopes in order to abandon themselves more completely to them.

'Quomodo fiet istud?' ('How can this be?').[39] This search is even more necessary because the christian attitude to evil lends itself to some very dangerous misunderstandings. A false interpretation of christian resignation, together with a false idea of christian detachment, is the principal source of the antagonisms which make so many Gentiles so sincerely hate the Gospel.

Let us ask ourselves now, and in what circumstances, our apparent deaths, that is, the waste-matter of our existence, can find their necessary place in the establishment, around us, of the divine milieu and the divine kingdom. It will help us to do this if we thoughtfully distinguish two phases, two periods, in the process which culminates in the transfiguration of our diminishments. The first of these phases is that of our struggle against evil, the second that of defeat and of its transfiguration.

A. *Our struggle with God against evil*

When christians suffer, they say 'God has touched us'. The words are pre-eminently true. But in their simplicity they summarize a complex series of spiritual operations only at the end of which do we have the right to speak these words. If, in the course of our encounters with evil, we try to distinguish what the medieval scholastics called 'the instants of nature', we shall, on the contrary, have to begin by saying 'God wants to free us from this diminishment—God wants us to help him take this cup away from us.'[40] To struggle against evil and to reduce to a minimum the evil (even the simply physical evil) which threatens us, is unquestionably the first act of

---

[39] *'Dixit autem Maria ad angelum quomodo fiet istud quoniam virum non cognosco'* ['Mary said to the angel, 'How can this be, since I do not know a man?'] (Lk 1.34 NKJ).
[40] Cf. 'Take this cup away from me' (Mk 14.36 NKJ).

our Father who is in heaven; it would be impossible to think of him—and even more impossible to love him—in any other way.

It is a perfectly correct view of things—and a view strictly in line with the Gospels—to consider providence across the ages as brooding over the world in a ceaseless effort to spare the world its wounds and to bind its injuries. Most certainly it is God himself who, over the centuries, awakens, in conformity with the general rhythm of progress, the great benefactors and the great physicians. He it is who inspires, even among the most convinced unbelievers, a quest for every means of comfort and every means of healing. Do we not acknowledge instinctively this divine presence when hatreds are quenched and their protesting uncertainty resolved as we kneel to thank each one of those who have helped our body or our mind to freedom? Can there be any doubt about it? At the first approach of the diminishments we cannot hope to find God except by loathing what is coming upon us and doing our best to avoid it. The more we repel suffering at this moment, with our whole heart and our whole strength,[41] the more closely we adhere to the heart and action of God.

B. *Our apparent failure and its transfiguration*

With God as our ally we are always certain of saving our souls. But we know too well that there is no guarantee that we shall always avoid suffering or even those interior defeats on account of which we can imagine our lives as failures. In any case, we are all growing old and we shall all die. This means that at one moment or another, no matter how well we resist, we shall feel the constraining grip of the forces

[41] Without bitterness and without revolt, of course, but with an anticipatory tendency to acceptance and final resignation. It is obviously difficult to separate the two 'instants of nature' without to some extent distorting them in describing them. But we should note: the necessity of this initial stage of resistance to evil is evident, and everyone admits it. The failure that follows on laziness, the illness contracted as a result of unjustified imprudence, could not be regarded by anyone as being the immediate will of God. (Author's Note.)

of diminishment, against which we have been fighting, gradually gaining mastery over the forces of life, and dragging us, physically vanquished, to the ground. But if God is for us, how can we be defeated? And what does this defeat mean?

The problem of evil, that is, the reconciling of our failures, even the purely physical ones, with creative goodness and creative power, will always remain for our hearts and minds one of the most disturbing mysteries of the universe. A full understanding of the suffering of creatures (like the pains of the damned) presupposes in us an appreciation of the nature and value of 'participated being' which, for lack of any point of comparison, we cannot have. Yet this much we can see: on the one hand, the work which God has undertaken in uniting himself intimately to created beings presupposes in them a slow preparation in the course of which they (who already exist, but are not yet complete) cannot of their nature avoid the risks (aggravated by an original fault) which are involved in the imperfect ordering of the multiple, in and around them; and on the other hand, because the final victory of good over evil can only be completed in the total organization of the world, our infinitely short individual lives cannot hope to know the joy, here below, of entry into the Promised Land. We are like soldiers who fall during an assault which leads to peace. God does not therefore suffer a preliminary defeat in our defeat because, although we appear to succumb individually, the world, in which we shall live again, triumphs in and through our deaths.

But this first aspect of his victory, which is enough to assure us of his omnipotence, is made complete by another disclosure, more direct perhaps, and in every case more immediately capable of being experienced by each of us, of his universal authority. By virtue of his very perfections,[42] God cannot ordain that the elements of a world in process of growth—or at least of a fallen world in process of rising

---

[42] Because his perfections cannot run counter to the nature of things, and because a world, assumed to be in process of perfection, or 'rising upwards', is of its nature precisely still partially disorganized. A world without a trace or threat of evil would be a world already consummated. (Author's Note.)

again—should avoid shocks and diminishments, even moral ones: *'necesse est enim ut veniant scandala'* ('It is necessary that temptations come').[43] But God will make it good—he will be avenged, we might say—by making evil itself serve a higher good of his faithful, the very evil which the present state of creation does not allow him to suppress immediately. Like artists who are able to make use of a fault or an impurity in the stone they are sculpting or the bronze they are casting to produce more exquisite lines or a more beautiful tone, God, without sparing us partial deaths, nor final death, which form an essential part of our lives, transfigures them by integrating them into a better plan, provided we lovingly trust in him. Not only our unavoidable ills, but our faults, even our most deliberate ones, can be embraced in this transformation, provided we always repent of them. Not everything is immediately good to those who seek God; but everything is capable of becoming good: *'omnia convertuntur in bonum'* ('all things turn to good').[44]

What is the process, what are the phases, by which God accomplishes this marvelous transformation of our deaths into a better life? By analogy with what we already know about achieving ourselves, and by reflection on what has always been the attitude and practical teaching of the Church on human suffering, we may hazard an answer to this question.

It could be said that providence, for those who believe in it, converts evil into good in three principal ways. Sometimes the failure we have undergone will divert our activity to more favorable objects or frameworks—though still situated on the level of the human goals we are pursuing. This is what happened with Job, whose final happiness was greater than his first. At other times, more often perhaps, the loss which afflicts us will compel us to find satisfaction of our

---

[43] Mt 18.7.

[44] For its more 'miraculous' effects, see the section on 'Faith' below. There is obviously no intention of giving a general theory of prayer here. (Author's Note.)

The Vulgate reads: *'omnia* cooperantur *in bonum'* ['all things work together for good'] (Rom 8.28). A more profound translation, which follows the Greek closely, would seem to be "God works together with those that love unto good in all things".

frustrated desires in less material fields, which neither worm nor rust can corrupt. The lives of the saints and, generally speaking, the lives of all those who have been outstanding for intelligence or goodness, are full of instances in which we can see them emerging ennobled, tempered and renewed from some ordeal, or even some downfall, which seemed bound to diminish or lay them low for ever. Failure then plays for us the part that the tail elevator plays for an aircraft or, if you prefer, the pruning knife for a plant. It canalizes the interior sap, it disengages the purest 'components' of our being in such a way as to make us shoot up higher and straighter. Collapse, even a moral one, is thus transformed into a success which, no matter how spiritual it may be, is still felt experientially. In the presence of S. Augustine, S. Mary Magdalene[45] or S. Lydwina,[46] no one hesitates to think *'felix dolor'* ('happy grief') or *'felix culpa'* ('happy fault').[47] With the result that, up to this point, we continue to 'understand' providence.

But there are more difficult cases (in fact, the most common ones) where human wisdom is altogether out of its depth. At every moment we see diminishments, both in and around us, which do not appear to be compensated by any advantage on any perceivable plane: premature deaths, stupid accidents, weaknesses affecting the highest reaches of our being. Under such blows, we do not move upwards in any perceptible direction; we disappear or remain grievously diminished. How can these diminishments which are altogether without compensation, in which we see death at its most deathly, become for us a good? This is where we can see in the domain of our diminishments a third way of action in which providence operates—a way that is the most effective and the most sanctifying of all.

---

[45] S. Mary of Magdala was one of the women who 'followed Jesus from Galilee' (Mt 27.55), one of the two Marys who discovered the empty tomb (Mk 16.1, 4–6; Lk 24.3), and the one to whom the Risen Christ first appeared (Mk 16.9).

[46] S. Lydwina of Schiedam (1380–1433), mystic.

[47] S. Augustine calls the Fall a 'happy fault' (*'felix culpa'*) because it made possible the incarnation. The words *'felix culpa'* are sung at the Easter Vigil.

God has already transfigured our sufferings by making them serve our conscious fulfillment. In his hands the forces of diminishment have perceptibly become the tool that cuts, sculpts and polishes within us the stone which is destined to occupy a precise place in the heavenly Jerusalem. He will do still more, because, as a result of his omnipotence encroaching upon our faith, events which show themselves experientially in our lives as pure loss will become an immediate factor in the union we dream of establishing with him.

Uniting ourselves means, in every case, migrating, dying partially in what we love. But if, as we believe, this annihilation in the other must be all the more complete the more we are attached to one who is greater than ourselves, we must ask what kind of uprooting is required for our journey into God. Doubtless, the progressive breaking-down of our egoism by the 'automatic' broadening of our human perspectives,[48] accompanied by the gradual spiritualization of our tastes and aspirations under the impact of certain setbacks, is a very real foretaste of the ecstasy which will save us from ourselves so that we may be subordinated to God. But the effect of this initial detachment is still only to develop to its utmost limits the center of our personality. Having arrived at this ultimate point we may still have the impression of possessing ourselves in a supreme degree—freer and more active than ever before. We have not yet crossed the critical threshold of our excentration, of our reversion to God. There is a further step to take: the one that makes us lose every foothold within ourselves—*'Illum oportet crescere me autem minui'* ('He must increase, but I must decrease').[49] We are still not lost to ourselves. What, then, will be the agent of this definitive transformation? Nothing less than death.

In itself, death is an incurable weakness of corporal beings, a weakness complicated in our world by the influence of an original fall. It is the sum and type of all the forces which diminish us, and against which we must fight without being able to hope for a

---

[48] See 'Detachment through action' above. (Author's Note.)
[49] Jn 3.30.

49

personal, direct and immediate victory. Now the great victory of the Creator and Redeemer, within our christian perspectives, is to have transformed what is in itself a universal power of diminishment and extinction into an essentially life-giving factor. God must, in some way or other, make room for himself, hollowing us out and emptying us, if he is finally to penetrate us. And to assimilate us in him, he must break the molecules of our being to re-cast and re-mold us. The function of death is to provide the necessary entrance into our innermost selves. It will make us undergo the required dissociation. It will put us into the state organically needed if the divine fire is to descend upon us. And in that way its fatal power to decompose and dissolve will be harnessed to the most sublime operations of life. What was, by nature, empty and void, a return to plurality, can become, in every human existence, fullness and unity in God.

C. *Communion through diminishment*

It was a joy to me, O God, in the midst of the struggle, to feel that in developing myself I was increasing the hold that you have upon me; it was a joy to me, too, under the interior thrust of life or amid the favorable play of events, to abandon myself to your providence. Now that I have found the joy of utilizing all forms of growth to make you, or to let you, grow in me, grant that I may willingly consent to this last phase of communication in the course of which I shall possess you by diminishing in you.

After having perceived you as the one who is 'a greater myself', grant, when my hour comes, that I may recognize you under the species of each alien or hostile force that seems bent upon destroying or uprooting me. When the signs of age begin to mark my body (and still more my mind); when the ill that is to diminish or carry me off strikes from without or is born within me; when the painful moment comes in which I suddenly awaken to the fact that I am ill or growing old; and above all at that last moment when I feel I am losing hold of myself and am absolutely passive in the hands of the great unknown energies that have formed me; in all those dark moments, O God, grant that I may understand that it is you (provided only my faith is strong enough) who are painfully parting the fibers of my being to penetrate to the very marrow of my substance and bear me away within yourself.

The more deeply and incurably the evil is encrusted in my flesh, the more it will be you that I am harboring, you as a loving, active principle of purification and detachment. The more the future is opened before me like some dizzy abyss or dark tunnel, the more confident I may be, if I venture forwards on the strength of your word, of losing myself and surrendering myself in you, of being assimilated by your body, Jesus.

O you who are energy of my Lord, you who are the irresistible and vivifying force, because, of the two of us, you are infinitely the stronger, it is on you that falls the role of consuming me in the union which must weld us together. Grant, therefore, something more precious still than the grace for which all the faithful pray. It is not enough that I should die while communicating. Teach me to communicate while dying.

D. *True resignation*

The analysis we have just made (in which we have tried to distinguish the phases by which our diminishments may be divinized) has allowed us to justify to ourselves the expression so comforting to those who suffer, 'God has touched me. God has taken away from me. His will be done.' Thanks to this analysis, we have understood how the two hands of God can reappear, more active and more penetrating than ever, beneath the evils which corrupt us from within, beneath the blows which break us up from without. But the same analysis has a further result, almost as priceless as the first. Corresponding to what we said earlier, it puts those of us who are christians in a position to justify to others the legitimacy and the human value of resignation.

There are many reasonable men and women who honestly consider and denounce christian resignation as being one of the most dangerous and soporific elements of the 'religious opium'.[50] Next to

---

[50] Teilhard was very conscious of the traditional marxist view that religion was 'the opium

disgust with the earth, there is no attitude which the Gospels are so
bitterly reproached with having encouraged as that of passivity in the
face of evil—a passivity which can go as far as the perverse cultiva-
tion of suffering and diminishment. As we have already said, with
reference to 'false detachment', this accusation, or even suspicion, is
infinitely more effective, at this moment, in preventing the conversion of the world than all the objections drawn from science or
philosophy. A religion which is judged to be inferior to our human
ideal, in spite of the marvels by which it is surrounded, is already
condemned. It is therefore of supreme importance for christians to
understand and live submissive to the will of God in the active sense
which, as we have said, is the only orthodox sense.

No, if they are to practice to the full the perfection of their christianity, christians must not falter in their duty to resist evil. On the
contrary, during the first phase, as we have seen, they must fight
sincerely and with all their might, in union with the creative force of
the world, to repel evil—so that nothing in or around them may be
diminished. During this initial phase, believers are the convinced
allies of all those who think that humanity will not succeed unless it
strives with all its might to realize its potentialities. And as we said
with reference to human development, believers are more closely
tied than anyone to this great task, because in their eyes the victory
of humanity over the diminishments of the world, even physical and
natural, conditions to some extent the fulfillment and consummation of the quite specific reality which they adore. As long as
resistance is possible, the children of heaven will resist, as firmly as
the most worldly children of the world, everything that deserves to
be scattered or destroyed.

Should they meet with defeat—the personal defeat which no
human being can ever hope to escape in its brief single combat with

of the people.' 'The only way of beating communism is to present Christ as he must be:
not as an opium (or a derivative), but as essential motive force (mover) of a hominization
which can only be completed energetically in a world which is amorized and open at the
summit' (Letter to Pierre Leroy SJ, 14 October 1952, *Lettres familières*, Centurion, 1976,
p. 164).

forces whose order of magnitude and evolution are universal—they, like the vanquished pagan heroes of old, will still maintain an interior resistance. Though they are stifled and constrained, their efforts will be sustained. At this point, however, they will see a new domain of possibilities opening out before them, instead of having nothing to compensate for and master their coming death except the melancholy and questionable consolation of stoicism (which, if carefully analyzed, would probably prove in the end to owe its beauty and consistency to a despairing faith in the value of sacrifice). This hostile force that crushes and disintegrates them can become for them a loving principle of renewal, if they accept it with faith while never ceasing to struggle against it. On the experiential plane, everything is lost. But in the domain of the so-called supernatural there is a further dimension which allows God to achieve, insensibly, a mysterious reversal of evil into good. Leaving the zone of human successes and failures behind them, christians accede by an effort of trust in the one greater than themselves to the region of supra-sensible transformations and growth. Their resignation is no more than the thrust which lifts the field of their activity higher.

We have come a long way, christianly speaking, from the justly criticized notion of 'submission to the will of God' which is in danger of weakening and softening the fine steel of the human will, brandished against all the powers of darkness and diminishment. Let us understand this well, and make it understood: finding and doing the will of God (even in diminishing and dying) implies neither a direct encounter nor a passive attitude. I have no right to think the evil that comes upon me through my own fault or negligence as being the touch of God.[51] I can only unite myself to the will of God (as endured passively) when all my strength is spent, at the point where my activity, fully extended and straining towards better-being (better-being understood in ordinary human terms), finds itself continually balanced by forces tending to halt or overwhelm me. Unless I do

---

[51] Though the harm which results from my negligence can become the will of God for me on condition I repent and correct my lazy or indifferent attitude of mind. Everything can be taken up again and recast in God, even one's faults. (Author's Note.)

everything I can to advance or resist, I shall not find myself at the required point—I shall not submit to God as much as I might have done or as much as he wishes. If, on the contrary, I persevere courageously, I shall rejoin God across evil, deeper down than evil; I shall draw close to him; and at this moment the optimum of my 'communion in resignation' necessarily coincides (by definition) with the maximum of fidelity to the human task.[52]

[52] In a letter written in late 1919 to his friend and confrère Auguste Valensin (1879–1953) Teilhard sets out his approach to spirituality:

'I agree fundamentally that the completion of the world can only be consummated through a death, a "night", a reversal, an excentration, a quasi-depersonalization ... Union with Christ supposes essentially that we transpose in him the ultimate center of our existence—something which implies a radical sacrifice of egoism ...

'The formula of renunciation, if it is to be total, must satisfy this double condition:

'1. It must make us go beyond everything there is in the world.

'2. And yet it must compel us, at the same time, to press forwards (with conviction and passion—because it is a question of life or death) the development of this same world. 'Christ gives himself to us through the world which is to be consummated (*etiam naturaliter*) in relation to him.

'You should note well: I attach no definitive or absolute value to the various human constructions. I like, not their particular form, but their function, which is to construct mysteriously, initially what can be divinized—and then, through the grace of Christ reposing on our effort, what is divine ...

'To sum up, complete christian effort consists, in my view, of three things:

'1. collaborating passionately in human effort, with an awareness that, not only through fidelity in obedience, but also through tasks accomplished, we are working towards the completion of the Pleroma by preparing the matter that is more or less to hand.

'2. achieving, in the course of this hard labor, and in the pursuit of an ever widening ideal, a preliminary form of renunciation and victory over a narrow and lazy egoism

'3. cherishing the "hollownesses" as well as the "fullnesses" of life—that is, its passivities and the providential diminishments through which Christ transforms "directly" and eminently into himself the elements and the personality which we have tried to develop for him ...

'Detachment and human effort are thereby harmonized ... their combinations are infinitely varied. There is an infinity of vocations, and, in every life, an infinity of phases. There are, within the Church, a S. Thomas Aquinas [*c.*1225–74] and a S. Vincent de Paul [1581–1660] side by side with a S. John of the Cross [1542–91]. There is, for each one of us, a time for growing and a time for diminishing. At one moment constructive human effort dominates, at another mystical annihilation ... All these attitudes proceed from the same interior orientation, from the same law which combines a double movement of the natural personalization of human beings and their supernatural depersonalization *in Christo*' (Letter to Auguste Valensin SJ, 12 December 1919, *Lettres intimes*, Aubier Montaigne, 1974, pp. 31, 33, 34, 35). (French Editor's Note.)

CONCLUSION TO PARTS ONE AND TWO
General Remarks on Christian Asceticism

Having observed the progressive invasion of divinization into the active and passive halves of our lives, we are now in a position to take a general view of the heavenly layers into which this tide of light has plunged us. This will form the third part of this work.

But before setting ourselves to contemplate the divine milieu, we must, for the sake of clarity, sum up in general terms the ascetic doctrine running through the preceding pages.

We shall do this in three sections under the following headings: (1) Attachment and detachment; (2) The sense of the Cross; (3) The spiritual power of matter.

1
Attachment and detachment

'Nemo dat quod non habet' ('no one gives what one does not have').[53] No sweet-smelling smoke without incense. No sacrifice without a victim. How could we give ourselves to God if he did not exist? What possession could he transfigure by his detachment if his hands were empty?

These common-sense observations enable us to solve, in principle, the question which is often formulated rather clumsily in the

---

[53] The Vulgate reads: *'si enim voluntas prompta est secundum id quod habet accepta est non secundum quod non habet'* ['For if there is first a willing mind, it is accepted according to what one has, and not according to what one does not have'] (2 Cor 8.12 NKJ).

following way: 'Which is better for christians: activity or passivity? Life or death? Growth or diminishment? Development or curtailment? Possession or renunciation?'

The general answer to this is: 'Why separate and contrast the two natural phases of a single effort? Your essential duty and desire is to be united with God. But in order to be united you must first of all be—and be yourselves as completely as possible. Develop yourselves and take possession of the world to be. Once this has been accomplished, then is the time to think about renunciation; then is the time to accept diminishment for the sake of being in another. Such is the sole and twofold precept of complete christian asceticism.'

Let us consider the two parts of this method more closely, and observe their particular interplay and the resulting effect.

A. *First, develop yourselves,*[54] *christianity says to christians*

Books on the spiritual life do not generally put this first phase of christian perfection into clear enough relief. Perhaps it seems too obvious to deserve mention, or seems to belong too completely to the 'natural' sphere, or possibly it seems too dangerous to be insisted upon—whatever the reason, these books usually remain silent on the subject or take it for granted. This is a fault and an omission. Although the majority of people understand it easily enough, and although its essentials are common to the ethics of both laity and

---

[54] The word 'First' clearly indicates a priority in nature as much as, or even more than, a priority in time. True christians should never purely and simply be attached to whatever it may be, because the contact they seek with things is always made with a view to transcending or transfiguring them. So that when we speak here of attachment, we mean something penetrated and dominated by detachment. However, the use and proportion of development in the spiritual life are particularly delicate matters, for nothing is easier than to pursue one's selfish interests under cover of growing and loving in God. The only real protection against the danger of illusion is a constant concern with keeping very much alive (with God's help) the impassioned vision of the One who is Greater than All. In the presence of this supreme interest, the very idea of growing or enjoying egotistically, for ourselves, becomes insipid, and intolerable. (Author's Note.)

religious, the duty of human perfection, like the whole universe, has been renewed, recast, supernaturalized, in the Kingdom of God. It is a truly christian duty to grow, even in the eyes of men and women, and to make one's talents bear fruit, even one's natural talents. It is part of the essentially catholic vision to look upon the world as maturing—not only in each individual or in each nation, but in the whole human race—a specific power of knowing and loving whose transfigured term is charity, but whose roots and elemental sap lie in the discovery and the love of everything that is true and beautiful in creation. This has already been explained with reference to the christian value of action; but here is the place to recall it: the effort of humanity, even in domains inaccurately called profane, must, in the christian life, assume the role of a holy and unifying operation. It is the collaboration, trembling with love, which we give to the hands of God, concerned to attire and prepare us (and the world) for the final union through sacrifice. Understood in this way, the care which we devote to personal achievement and embellishment is no more than a gift begun. And that is why the attachment to creatures which it appears to denote melts imperceptibly into complete detachment.

B. *And if you possess anything, Christ says in the Gospels, leave it and follow me* [55]

Up to a certain point believers who, understanding the christian meaning of development, have worked to mold themselves and the world for God, will hardly need to hear the second injunction before beginning to obey it. Those whose aim, in conquering the earth, has really been to subject a little more matter to spirit have, surely, begun to take leave of themselves at the same time as taking possession of themselves. This is also true of those who reject mere enjoyment, the line of least resistance, the easy possession of things and ideas, and set out courageously on the path of work, interior renewal and the

[55] Cf. Mt 19.21; Mk 10.21; Lk 18.22.

ceaseless broadening and purification of their ideal. And it is true, again, of those who have given their time, their health, or their lives, to something greater than themselves—a family to be supported, a country to be saved, a truth to be discovered, a cause to be defended. All these are continually passing from attachment to detachment as they faithfully mount the ladder of human effort.

There are, however, two reserved forms of renunciation upon which christians will only embark at the invitation or on the express order of their Creator. We refer to the practice of evangelical counsels and the use of diminishments, neither of which is justified by the pursuit of a clearly defined higher good.

Where the first form is concerned, no-one will deny that the religious life (which was also discovered, and is still practiced, outside of christianity) can be a normal and 'natural' flowering of human activity in search of a higher life. However the practice of the virtues of poverty, chastity and obedience does represent the beginnings of a flight beyond the normal spheres of earthly, procreative and conquering humanity; and for this reason they had to wait, before becoming generally valid and licit, for a *'duc in altum'* ('Put out into deep water')[56] to authenticate the aspirations maturing in the human soul. This authorization was given once and for all in the Gospels by the master of things. But it must also be heard individually by those who are to benefit from it: it is 'vocation'.

With the practice of the forces of diminishment, the initiative must, even more clearly, come entirely from God. We can and should make use of penances of some kind to organize the hierarchy of, and liberate, the lower powers within us. We can and should sacrifice ourselves when a greater interest claims us. But we do not have the right to diminish ourselves simply for the sake of diminishing ourselves. Voluntary mutilation, even when conceived as a method of interior liberation, is a crime against being, and christianity has always explicitly condemned it. The most firmly established teaching of the Church is that it is our duty as creatures to try and live more

---

[56] Lk 5.4.

and more by the higher parts of ourselves, in conformity with the aspirations of the present life. This alone is our concern. All the rest belongs to the wisdom of the one who alone can bring forth another life from every form of death.

There is no need to be wildly impatient. The master of death will come soon enough—and perhaps we can already hear his footsteps. There is no need to forestall his hour, nor to fear it. When he enters into us to destroy, as it seems, the virtues and the forces that we have distilled with so much loving care out of the sap of the earth, it will be as a loving fire to consummate our completion in union.

C. Development and renunciation, attachment and detachment, are not mutually exclusive

Hence, in the general rhythm of christian life, development and renunciation, attachment and detachment, are not mutually exclusive. On the contrary, they harmonize, like breathing in and out of our lungs. They are two phases of the soul's breath, or two components of the impulse by which the christian life uses things as a springboard from which to go beyond them.[57]

This is the general solution. In the detail of particular cases, the sequence of these two phases and the combinations of these two components are subject to an infinite number of subtle variations. Their exact blending calls for a spiritual tact which is the strength and virtue proper to the masters of the interior life. In some christians

---

[57] From this 'dynamic' point of view the opposition so often stressed between asceticism and mysticism disappears. There is nothing in our concern for personal self-perfection to distract us from our absorption in God, provided this ascetic effort is simply the beginning of 'mystical annihilation'. There is no longer any reason to distinguish between an (ascetic) 'anthropomorphism' and a (mystical) 'theocentricism' once the human center is seen and loved in conjunction with (that is, in movement towards) the divine center. Of course as God takes possession of us, the creature finally becomes passive (because it finds itself super-created in the divine union). But this passivity presupposes a subject that reacts, that is, an active phase. The fire of heaven must come down on something: otherwise there would be nothing consumed and nothing consummated. (Author's Note.)

detachment will always retain the form of disinterestedness and effort which belongs to human work faithfully carried out: the transfiguration of life will be wholly interior. In others a physical or moral breach will occur in the course of their lives which will cause them to pass from the level of a very holy normal life to the level of elected renunciations and mystical states. But for all of them, in any event, the road ends at the same point: the final stripping in death which accompanies the recasting, and is a prelude to final incorporation, *in Christo Iesu*.[58] And for all of them again, what makes or mars their life is the degree of harmony with which the two factors of growing for Christ, and diminishing in him, are combined in the light of the natural and supernatural aptitudes involved. It would clearly be as absurd to prescribe unlimited development or renunciation as it would be to set no bounds to eating or fasting. In the spiritual life, as in all organic processes, everyone has their optimum and it is just as harmful to go beyond it as not to attain it.[59]

What has been said of individuals must be transposed and applied to the Church as a whole. It is probable that the Church has been led, at different times in the course of its existence, to emphasize in its general life, on some occasions, a greater care to collaborate in the earthly task, on others, a more jealous concern to stress the ultimate transcendence of its preoccupations. What is quite certain is that its health and integrity, at any given moment, depend upon the exactitude with which its members, each in their

---

[58] Rom 3.24.

[59] One thus evades the basic problem of the use of creatures if one solves it by saying that in all cases the least possible should be taken from them. This minimum theory is no doubt the product of the mistaken idea that God grows in us by destruction or substitution rather than by transformation or, which comes to the same thing, that the spiritual potential of the material creation is now exhausted. The minimum theory may be useful in reducing certain apparent risks; but it does not teach us how to get the maximum spiritual yield from the objects which surround us—which is what the reign of God really means. The one absolute rule upon which we can depend in this matter would seem to be this: 'To love in the world, in God, something which may always become greater.' All the rest is a matter of christian prudence and individual vocation. See below under 'The spiritual power of matter' where we discuss the utilization by each one of us of the spiritual powers of matter. (Author's Note.)

proper place, fulfill their functions which range from the duty of applying themselves to what are reputed to be the most profane of worldly occupations, to vocations which call for the most austere penances or the most sublime contemplation. All these roles are necessary. The Church is like a great tree whose roots must be energetically anchored in the earth while its leaves are serenely exposed to the bright sunlight. In this way at every moment it sums up a whole range of innumerable pulsations in a single living act of synthesis, each one of which corresponds to a particular degree or possible form of spiritualization.

In the midst of all that diversity there is, however, something which dominates—something which confers its distinctively christian character on the organism as a whole (as well as upon each element within it): it is the impulse towards heaven, the laborious and painful bursting out beyond matter. It is important to remember (and we have not finished insisting on this point) that the supernatural awaits and sustains the progress of our nature. But it must not be forgotten that it only purifies and perfects that progress, in the end, in an apparent annihilation. The inseparable alliance between the two parts, personal progress and renunciation in God; but also the continual, and then final, ascendancy of the second over the first— it is these that sum up the full sense of the mystery of the Cross.

2
The sense of the Cross [60]

The Cross has always been a sign of contradiction, and a principle of selection, among men and women. Faith tells us that it is by the willed attraction or repulsion exercised upon souls by the Cross that the sorting of the good seed from the bad, the separation of the chosen elements from the unusable ones, is accomplished at the heart of humanity. Wherever the Cross appears, unrest and antago-

---

[60] Teilhard uses 'sense' here to suggest both 'meaning' and 'direction'.

nisms are inevitable. But there is no reason why these conflicts should needlessly be exacerbated by preaching the doctrine of Jesus Crucified in a discordant or provocative manner. Far too often the Cross is presented for our adoration, not so much as a sublime end to be attained by our transcending ourselves, but as a symbol of sadness, limitation, and repression.

This way of preaching the Passion is, in many cases, simply the result of the clumsy use of a pious vocabulary in which the most solemn words (such as sacrifice, immolation, expiation), emptied of their meaning by routine, are used, quite unconsciously, in a light and frivolous way. They become formulas to be juggled with. But this manner of speech ends by conveying the impression that the Kingdom of God can only be established in mourning, and by thwarting and going against the current of human aspirations and energies. In spite of the verbal fidelity displayed by the use of this kind of language, nothing is less christian than such a picture. What we said just now about the necessary combination of attachment and detachment allows us to give christian asceticism a much richer and a far more complete meaning.

In its highest and most general sense, the doctrine of the Cross is what all adhere to who believe that the vast movement and agitation of human life opens on to a road which leads somewhere—and which climbs upwards. Life has a term: therefore it imposes a particular direction, orientated, in fact, towards the highest possible spiritualization through the greatest possible effort. To admit this group of fundamental principles is already to range ourselves among the disciples—distant, perhaps, and implicit, but real—of Jesus Crucified. Once this first choice has been made, the first distinction has been drawn between the courageous who will succeed and the pleasure-seekers who will fail, between the elect and the condemned.

This still rather vague attitude is clarified and carried further by christianity. Above all, by revealing an original fall, christianity provides our intelligence with a reason for the disconcerting excess of sin and suffering at certain points. Next, to win our love and secure our faith, it unveils to our minds and hearts the moving and unfathomable reality of the historical Christ in whom the exemplary life of an individual man conceals this mysterious drama: the master of the world, leading, like an element of the world, not only an elemental life, but (in addition to this and because of it) leading the total life of the universe, which he has shouldered and assimilated by experiencing it himself. And finally by the crucifixion and death of his adored being, christianity signifies to our thirst for happiness that the term of creation is not to be sought in the temporal zones of our visible world, but that the effort required of our fidelity must be consummated beyond a total metamorphosis of ourselves and of everything surrounding us.

Thus the perspectives of renunciation implicit in the exercise of life itself are gradually expanded. Ultimately we find ourselves thoroughly uprooted, as the Gospels wish, from everything tangible on earth. But this process of uprooting ourselves has occurred little by little, following a rhythm which has neither alarmed nor wounded the respect we owe to the admirable beauties of the human effort.

It is perfectly true that the Cross means going beyond the frontiers of the sensible world and even, in a sense, breaking with it. The final stages of the ascent to which it calls us compel us to cross a threshold, a critical point, where we lose touch with the zone of the realities of the senses. This final 'excess', glimpsed and accepted from the first steps, inevitably puts everything we do in a special light and gives it a particular significance. This is exactly where the folly of christianity lies in the eyes of the 'wise' who are not prepared to stake the good which they now hold in their hands on a total 'beyond'. But this agonizing flight from the experiential zones, which is what the Cross means, is only (as should be strongly emphasized) the sublime aspect of a law common to all life. Towards the peaks, shrouded in mist from our human eyes, towards which the Cross beckons us, we rise by a path which is the way of universal progress. The royal road of the Cross is no more and no less than the road of human effort supernaturally righted and prolonged. Once we have fully grasped the sense of the Cross, we are no longer in danger of finding life sad and ugly. We shall simply have become more attentive to its barely comprehensible solemnity.

To sum up, Jesus on the Cross is both the symbol and the reality of the immense labor of the centuries which, little by little, has raised up the created spirit and brought it back to the depths of the divine milieu. He represents (and in a true sense, he is) creation, as, upheld by God, it re-ascends the slopes of being, sometimes clinging to things for support, sometimes tearing itself from them to pass beyond them, and always compensating, by physical suffering, for the setbacks caused by its moral downfalls.

The Cross is not, therefore, something inhuman, but super-human. We can now understand that from the very first, from the very origins of humanity as we know it, the Cross was placed on the crest of the road which leads to the highest peaks of creation. But, in the growing light of Revelation, its arms which at first were bare, show themselves to have put on Christ: *'Crux inuncta'* ('the anointed Cross'). At first sight the bleeding body may seem funereal to us. Is it not from the night that it shines forth? But if we go nearer we shall recognize the flaming Seraph of Alvernia[61] whose passion and compassion are *'incendium mentis'* ('the embrace of the spirit'). Christians are asked to live, not in the shadow of the Cross, but in the fire of its creative action.[62]

3
The spiritual power of matter

The same beam of light which christian spirituality, rightly under-stood, directs upon the Cross to humanize it (without veiling it) is reflected on matter to spiritualize it.

---

[61] In the summer of 1224 S. Francis (1181–1226) went to the mountain retreat of La Verna, not far from Assisi. As he prayed one morning, at the time of the Feast of the Exaltation of the Cross (14 September), he had a vision of the heavenly figure who has come down to us as the Seraph of Alvernia.
[62] In an essay of 1918—not intended like *The Divine Milieu* for 'the waverers, both inside

In their struggle towards the mystical life, men and women have often succumbed to the illusion of crudely contrasting good and evil, body and soul, spirit and flesh. But despite certain current expressions, this manichaean[63] tendency has never been approved by the Church. And, to prepare the way for our final view of the divine milieu, we might be allowed perhaps to vindicate and exalt that aspect which the Lord came to put on, save and consecrate: namely, holy matter.

Matter, from the mystical or ascetic point of view we have adopted in these pages, is not exactly any of the abstract entities defined under this name by science or philosophy. It is certainly the

and outside'—Teilhard freely expressed, in the course of a meditation, the capital importance he attached to the priestly and religious vocation, to the evangelical counsels, and to the redemptive power of death:

'Every priest, because he is a priest, has dedicated his life to the work of universal salvation. If he is conscious of the dignity of his vocation, he should no longer live for himself, but for the world, following the example of the one whom he is anointed to represent . . .

'To the full extent of my strength, because I am a priest, I want from now on to be the first to become conscious of everything the world loves, pursues and suffers; first to seek, to sympathize, and to suffer; the first to open myself out and sacrifice myself—to become more widely human and more nobly of the earth than of any servant of the world . . .

'And I wish, at the same time, by practicing the counsels, to recover through renunciation everything there may be of heavenly fire in the threefold concupiscence—sanctifying, through chastity, poverty, and obedience, the power invested in love, in gold, and in independence . . .

'*Was there ever a humanity, O Lord, more like, in its blood, an immolated victim,—more adapted, in its interior agitation, to creative transformations,—richer, in its violence, in sanctifiable energy,—closer, in its anguish, to supreme communion? . . .*

'O Priests . . . who have never been priests in a fuller sense than you are now, merged and submerged as you are in the pain and blood of a whole generation,—never more active,—never more directly in line with your vocation . . .

'*I feel so weak, Lord, that I hardly dare ask you to let me participate in this Beatitude. But I see it clearly and I shall proclaim it: "Happy are they among us who in these decisive days of Creation and Redemption are chosen for this supreme act, the logical crowning of their priesthood: communion unto death with the Christ who is being born and suffering in the human race!"*' ('Le Prêtre' (1918), *Écrits du temps de la guerre*, Seuil, 1976, pp. 328, 331, 332, 333 (our translation); cf. 'The Priest' (1918), *Writings in Time of War*, Collins, 1968, pp. 219, 222, 223–4.) (French Editor's Note.)
[63] Manichaeism: a dualistic religion long condemned by the Church, based on a supposed conflict between light and darkness, good and evil, founded by Mani (or Manes) in Mesopotamia in the third century. S. Augustine professed manichaeism for nine years before his conversion.

same concrete reality, for us, as it is for physics or metaphysics, having the same basic attributes of plurality, tangibility and inter-connectedness. But here we want to embrace this reality as a whole in its widest possible sense: to give it its full abundance as it reacts not only to our scientific or analytical investigations, but to all our practical activities. Matter, as far as we are concerned, is the assemblage of things, energies and creatures which surround us to the extent that these are palpable, sensible and 'natural' (in the theological sense of the word). Matter is the common milieu, universal and tangible, infinitely shifting and varied, in which we live.

How, then, does the thing so defined present itself to us to be acted upon? Under the enigmatic features of a two-sided power.

On the one hand, matter is the burden, the fetters, the pain, the sin and the threat to our lives. It is what weighs us down, what suffers, wounds, tempts and grows old. Matter makes us heavy, paralyzed, vulnerable, guilty. Who will deliver us from this body of death?

But matter, at the same time, is physical exuberance, ennobling contact, virile effort, the joy of growth. It is what attracts, renews, unites and flowers. By matter we are nourished, lifted up, linked to everything else, invaded by life. To be deprived of it is intolerable: *'non nolumus expoliari sed supervestiri'* ('we wish not to be unclothed but to be further clothed').[64]

Asceticism deliberately looks no further than the first aspect, the one which is turned towards death; and it recoils, exclaiming 'Flee!' *But what would our spirits be, O God, if they did not have the bread of earthly things to nourish them, the wine of created beauties to intoxicate them, and the conflicts of human life to fortify them? What feeble energies and bloodless hearts your creatures would bring you if they were to succeed in cutting themselves off prematurely from the providential setting in which you have placed them! Teach us, Lord, how to contemplate the sphinx without succumbing to its spell; how to grasp the hidden mystery in the womb of death, not by a refinement of human doctrine, but in the simple concrete act by which you plunged yourself into mat-*

---

[64] 2 Cor 5.4. (New Jerusalem Bible.)

66

ter to redeem it. By the virtue of your suffering Incarnation disclose to us, and then teach us to harness jealously for you, the spiritual power of matter.

Let us take a comparison as our starting point. Imagine a deep-sea diver trying to get back from the seabed to the clear light of day. Or imagine a traveler on a fog-bound mountainside climbing upwards towards the summit bathed in light. For both space is divided into two zones marked with opposing properties: the one behind and beneath appears ever darker, while the one in front and above becomes ever lighter. Both diver and climber can succeed in making their way towards the second zone only if they use everything around and about them as points of leverage. Moreover, in the course of their task, the light above them grows brighter with each advance made; and at the same time the area which has been traversed, to the extent that it is traversed, ceases to hold the light and is engulfed in darkness. Let us remember these stages, for they express symbolically all the elements we need to understand how we should touch and handle matter with a proper sense of reverence.

Matter, above all, is not just the weight that drags us down, the mire that sucks us in, the bramble that bars our way. In itself, and before we find ourselves where we are, and before we choose, it is simply the slope on which we can go up just as well as go down, the milieu that can uphold or give way, the wind that can overthrow or lift up. Of its nature, and as a result of original sin, it is true that it represents a perpetual impulse towards failure. But by nature too, and as a result of the Incarnation, it contains the spur or the allurement to be our accomplice towards greater-being, and this counter-balances and even dominates the *'fomes peccati'* ('the tinder for sin').[65] The full truth of our situation is that, here below, and by virtue of our immersion in the universe, each one of us is placed within its layers or on its slopes, at a specific point defined by the present moment in the history of the world, the place of our birth, and our individual vocation. And from that starting point, variously situated at different

---

[65] 'Concupiscence, or, metaphorically, "the tinder for sin" (*fomes peccati*).' (*Catechism of the Catholic Church*, Geoffrey Chapman, 1994, § 1264.)

levels, the task assigned to us is to climb towards the light, passing through, to attain God, a given series of created things which are not exactly obstacles but rather foot-holds, intermediaries to be made use of, nourishment to be taken, sap to be purified and elements to be associated with us and borne along with us.

That being so, and still as a result of our initial position among things, and also as a result of each position we subsequently occupy in matter, matter falls into two distinct zones, differentiated according to our effort: the zone already left behind or arrived at, to which we should not return, or at which we should not pause, lest we fall back—this is the zone of matter in the material and carnal sense; and the zone offered to our renewed efforts towards progress, search, conquest and 'divinization', the zone of matter taken in the spiritual sense. And the frontier between these two zones is essentially relative and shifting. What is good, sanctifying and spiritual for my brothers and sisters below or beside me on the mountain side, can be material, misleading or bad for me. What I rightly allowed myself yesterday, I must perhaps deny myself today. And conversely, actions which would have been a grave betrayal in a S. Aloysius Gonzaga[66] or a S. Anthony,[67] may well be models for me if I am to follow in the footsteps of these saints. In other words, the soul can only rejoin God after having traversed a specific path through matter, which path can be seen as the distance which separates, but also as the road which connects. Without certain possessions and certain victories, none of us exists as God wishes us to be. We each have our Jacob's ladder,[68] whose rungs are formed of a series of objects. Thus it is not our business to withdraw from the world before our time; rather let us learn to orientate our being in the flux of things; then, instead of the force of gravity which drags us down to the abyss of self-indulgence and selfishness, we shall feel a salutary 'component' emerging from created things which, by a process we have already described, will enlarge our horizons, will snatch us

---

[66] S. Aloysius Gonzaga (1568–91).
[67] Probably S. Anthony of Padua OFM (c.1193–1231).
[68] Gen 28.12.

away from our pettinesses and impel us imperiously towards a widening of our vision, towards the renunciation of cherished pleasures, towards the desire for ever more spiritual beauty. Matter, which at first seemed to counsel us towards the maximum pleasure and the minimum effort, emerges as the principle of minimum pleasure and maximum effort.

In this case, too, the law of the individual would seem to be a small-scale version of the law of the whole. It would surely not be far wrong to suggest that, in its universality, the world too has a prescribed path to follow before attaining its consummation. There is no doubt about it. If the material totality of the world includes unusable energies; and if, more unfortunately, it contains perverted energies and elements which are slowly separating from it, it is still more certain that it contains a certain quantity of spiritual power of which the progressive sublimation *in Christo Iesu* [69] is, for the Creator, the fundamental operation taking place. At the present time this power is still diffused almost everywhere: nothing, however insignificant or crude it may appear, is without some trace of it. And the task of the Body of Christ, living in his faithful, is patiently to sort out those heavenly forces—to extract, without letting any of it be lost, that chosen substance. Little by little, we can be certain, the work continues. Thanks to the multitude of individuals and vocations, the Spirit of God insinuates itself and is at work everywhere. It is the great tree we spoke of a moment ago, whose sunlit branches refine and turn to flower the sap extracted by the humblest of its roots. As the work progresses, certain zones probably become exhausted. Within each individual life, as we have noted, the frontier between spiritual matter and carnal matter is constantly moving upwards. And in the same way, as humanity is christianized, it feels less and less need for certain earthly nourishment. Contemplation and chastity should thus tend, quite legitimately, to gain mastery over anxious work and direct possessions. This is the general 'drift' of matter towards spirit. This movement must have its term. One day the

[69] Rom 3.24.

whole divinizable substance of matter will have passed into our souls; all the chosen dynamisms will have been recovered: and then our world will be ready for the Parousia.[70]

Who can fail to recognize the great symbolic gesture of baptism in this general history of matter? Christ immerses himself in the waters of Jordan, symbol of the energies of the earth. He sanctifies them. And as he emerges, says S. Gregory of Nyssa,[71] he elevates the whole world with the water which runs off his body.

Immersion and emergence; participation in things and sublimation; possession and renunciation; crossing through and being borne onwards—that is, the twofold yet single movement which answers the challenge of matter to save it.[72]

Matter, seductive and strong, matter, which caresses and makes virile, matter which enriches and destroys—with faith in the heavenly influences which have sweetened and purified your waters—I surrender myself to your mighty layers. The virtue of Christ has passed into you. May your attractions lead me onwards, may your sap nourish me; may your resistance toughen me; may your uprooting free me. And, finally, may your whole being divinize me.

---

[70] Teilhard understands the Parousia as the 'Presence of Christ in glory at the end of time bringing together the final center, Omega, who is the term of the phenomenal world, and Christ-Omega, who consummates the totality of creation in the completion of his Mystical Body' (*The Teilhard Lexicon*, p. 146).

[71] S. Gregory of Nyssa (*c.*335–*c.*395), younger brother of S. Basil the Great of Cæsarea (*c.*329–379), bishop of Nyssa (371), one of the three 'Great Hierarchs'.

[72] The sensual mysticisms and certain neo-pelagianisms (such as Americanism), by paying too much attention to the first of these phases, have fallen into the error of seeking divine love and the divine kingdom on the same level as human affections and human progress. Conversely, by concentrating too much on the second phase, some exaggerated forms of christianity conceive perfection as built upon the destruction of 'nature'. The true christian supernatural, frequently defined by the Church, neither leaves creatures where they are, on their own plane, nor suppresses them: rather it super-animates them. It must surely be obvious that, however transcendent and creative they may be, God's love and ardor could only fall upon the human heart, that is, upon an object prepared (from near or far) by means of all the nourishments of the earth. It is astonishing that so few minds should succeed, in this as in other cases, in grasping the notion of transformation. Sometimes the thing transformed seems to them to be the old thing unchanged; at other times they see in it only the entirely new. In the first case it is spirit that eludes them; in the second, it is matter. Though not so crude as the first excess, the second is shown by experience to be no less destructive of human equilibrium. (Author's Note.)

PART THREE

The Divine Milieu

Nemo sibi vivit, aut sibi moritur . . .
Sive vivimus, sive morimur, Christi sumus.
We do not live or die to ourselves.
But, whether through our life or through our death, we belong to Christ.[73]

The first two parts of this study are no more than an analysis and verification of S. Paul's words. We have considered, in turn, the sphere of activity, development and life, and the sphere of passivities, diminishment and death. All around us, to right and to left, before and behind, above and below, we have only had to go a little beyond the frontier of sensible appearances to see the divine welling up and shining through. But it is not only close to us, in front of us, that the divine presence is revealing itself. It has sprung up so universally, and we find ourselves so surrounded and transfixed by it, that there is no room left to fall down on our knees and worship it—even within ourselves.

By means of all created things, without exception, the divine assails, penetrates and molds us. We thought it distant and inaccessible, whereas in fact we live steeped in its burning layers: *'in eo vivimus'* ('in him we live').[74] In truth, as Jacob said, awakening from his dream, the world, this palpable world, which we were used to treating with the boredom and disrespect with which we habitually regard places with no sacred association, is a holy place, and we did not know it.[75] *'Venite adoremus'* ('O Come, let us worship').[76]

---

[73] The Vulgate reads: *'Nemo enim nostrum sibi vivit et nemo sibi moritur sive enim vivimus Domino vivimus sive morimur Domino morimur sive ergo vivimus sive morimur Domini sumus'* ['We do not live to ourselves, and we do not die to ourselves. If we live, we live to the Lord, and if we die, we die to the Lord; so then, whether we live or whether we die, we are the Lord's'] (Rom 14.7–8).
[74] Acts 17.28 NKJ.

Let us withdraw to the upper spiritual atmosphere which bathes us in living light. And let us rejoice in making an inventory of its attributes and recognizing their nature, before examining in a general way the means by which we can open ourselves more and more to its penetration.

1

Attributes of the divine milieu

The essential marvel of the divine milieu is the ease with which it assembles and harmonizes within itself qualities which appear to us the most contradictory.

As vast as the world and much more formidable than the most immense energies of the universe, the divine milieu possesses to a supreme degree the concentration and precision which make up the warmth and charm of human persons.

Vast and innumerable as the scintillating surge of creatures which its ocean sustains and super-animates, it retains at the same time the concrete transcendence that allows it to bring back the elements of the world, without the least confusion, within its triumphant and personal unity.

Incomparably near and tangible, since it presses in upon us through all the forces of the universe, it eludes however our grasp so constantly that we can never seize it here below except by raising ourselves, uplifted on its waves, to the extreme limit of our effort: present in and drawing at the inaccessible depth of each creature, it always withdraws further, carrying us with it towards the common center of all consummation.[77]

Through it, the touch of matter purifies and chastity flowers as the sublimation of love.

---

[75] 'Then Jacob woke from his sleep and said, "Surely the Lord is in this place—and I did not know it!"' (Gen 28.16).

[76] Ps 94.6 (Vulgate). Ps 94.6 in the Vulgate is Ps 95.6 in modern translations.

[77] I attain God in those whom I love to the same degree in which we, myself and they,

In it, development culminates in renunciation. Attachment to things separates us from everything disintegrating within them. Death becomes a resurrection.

Now, if we try to discover the source of so many astonishingly coupled perfections, we shall find they all spring from the same 'fontal' property which we can express as follows: God reveals himself everywhere, beneath our groping efforts, as a universal milieu, only because he is the ultimate point upon which all realities converge. Each element of the world, whatever it may be, only subsists, *hic et nunc*, in the manner of a cone[78] whose generatrices meet in God who draws them together (meeting at the term of their individual perfection and at the term of the general perfection of the world which contains them). It follows that all creatures, everyone of them, cannot be considered in their nature and action without the same reality being found in their most interior being—like sunlight in the fragments of a broken mirror—one[79] beneath its multiplicity, unattainable beneath its proximity, spiritual beneath its materiality. No object can influence us by its essence without our being touched by the radiance of the universal focus. Our hearts, minds and hands are incapable of grasping what is essentially desirable in reality without our being compelled by the very structure of things to go back to the first source of its perfections. This focus, this source, is everywhere. It is precisely because he is infinitely profound and punctiform[80] that God is infinitely close yet present everywhere. It is precisely because he is the center that he fills the whole sphere. Exactly because it is the opposite of this fallacious ubiquity which matter seems to derive from its extreme dissociation, the divine omnipresence is simply the effect of its extreme spirituality. And in

---

become more and more spiritual. In the same way, I grasp him in the Beautiful and the Good as I pursue these further and further with progressively purified faculties. (Author's Note.)

[78] Teilhard frequently expresses 'the convergent acceleration of organic time using the image of a cone converging towards the summit' (*The Teilhard Lexicon*, p. 193).

[79] See footnote 2, p. 1, for an explanation of 'one'.

[80] *Punctiform*, having the form of a point.

the light of this discovery, we may resume our march through the inexhaustible wonders which the divine milieu has in store for us.

The divine milieu, no matter how large it is, is in reality a center. It has therefore the properties of a center, that is, above all, the absolute and final power to unite (and consequently to complete) all beings within itself. In the divine milieu all the elements of the universe touch each other by what is most interior and ultimate in them. There they concentrate, little by little, all that is purest and most attractive in them without loss and without danger of subsequent corruption. There they shed, in their meeting, the mutual exteriority and incoherences which form the basic pain of human relationships. Let those seek refuge there who are saddened by the separations, the meanness and the wastefulness of the world! In the external spheres of the world, we are always torn by the separations which set distance between bodies, which set the impossibility of mutual understanding between souls, which set death between lives. Moreover at every minute we must lament that we cannot pursue and embrace everything within the space of a few years. Finally, and not without reason, we are incessantly distressed by the crazy indifference and the heartbreaking dumbness of a natural environment in which the greater part of individual effort seems wasted or lost, where the blows and cries seem stifled on the spot, without awakening any echo.

All that is only desolation on the surface.

But let us leave the surface. And, without leaving the world, let us plunge into God. There and from there, in him and through him, we shall hold all things and have command of all things. There we shall one day rediscover the essence and brilliance of all the flowers and lights which we were forced to abandon to be faithful to life. The beings we despaired of reaching and influencing are all there, all reunited by the most vulnerable, receptive and enriching point in their substance. In this place the least of our desires and efforts is harvested and tended and can at any moment cause the marrow of the universe to vibrate.

Let us establish ourselves in the divine milieu. There we shall find ourselves where the soul is most deep and where matter is most dense. There we shall discover, where all its beauties flow together, the ultra-vital, the ultra-sensitive, the ultra-active point of the universe. And, at the same time, we shall feel the plenitude of our powers of action and adoration effortlessly ordered within our deepest selves.

But the fact that all the external springs of the world should be coordinated and harmonized at that privileged point is not the only marvel. By a complementary marvel, those who abandon themselves to the divine milieu feel it clearly directs and vastly expands their interior powers with a sureness which enables them to avoid, like child's play, the numerous reefs on which mystical ardor has so often foundered.

In the first place, the sojourner in the divine milieu is no pantheist. At first sight, perhaps, the depths of the divine which S. Paul shows us may seem to resemble the fascinating domains unfolded before our eyes by monistic philosophies or religions. In fact they are very different, far more reassuring to our minds, far more comforting to our hearts. Pantheism seduces us by its vistas of perfect universal union. But ultimately, if it were true, it would give us only fusion and unconsciousness; for, at the end of the evolution it claims to reveal, the elements of the world vanish in the God they create or by which they are absorbed. Our God, on the contrary, pushes to its furthest possible limit the differentiation among the creatures he concentrates within himself. At the peak of their adherence to him, the elect also discover in him the consummation of their individual fulfillment. Christianity alone therefore saves, with the rights of thought, the essential aspiration of all mysticism: to be united (that is, to become the other) while remaining ourselves. More attractive than any world-Gods, whose eternal seduction it embraces, transcends and purifies— *'in omnibus omnia Deus' (En pôsi panta Theos)* ('God all in all')[81]—our divine milieu is at the antipodes of false pantheism. Christians can plunge themselves into it whole-heartedly without risk of finding themselves one day a monist.[82]

---

[81] The Vulgate reads: *'ut sit Deus omnia in omnibus'* ['so that God may be all in all'] (1 Cor 15.28).

Nor is there any reason to fear that in abandoning themselves to those deep waters, they will lose their foothold in revelation and in life, that is, become either unrealistic in the object of their worship or else chimerical in the substance of their work. Christians lost within the divine layers will not find their mind subject to the forbidden distortions that go to make the 'modernists'[83] or the 'illuminati'.[84]

To the christians' sensitized vision, it is true, the Creator and, more precisely, the Redeemer (as we shall see) have steeped themselves in all things and penetrated all things to such a degree that, as S. Angela of Foligno said, 'the world is full of God'.[85] But this augmentation is only valuable in their eyes to the extent that the light, in which everything seems to them bathed, radiates from an historical center and is transmitted along a traditional and solidly defined axis. The immense enchantment of the divine milieu owes all its value in the long run to the human–divine contact which was revealed at the Epiphany of Jesus. If we suppress the historical reality of Christ, the divine omnipresence which intoxicates us becomes, like all the other dreams of metaphysics, uncertain, vague, conventional—lacking the decisive experiential verification by which to impose itself on our minds, and without the moral authority to assimilate our lives into it. From now on, no matter how dazzling the expansions which we shall try in a moment to discern in the resurrected Christ, their beauty and their stuff of reality will always remain inseparable from the tangible

[82] *Monist*, one who holds that there is no difference in substance between matter and spirit. 'All forms of monism are in conflict with the christian belief in a radical distinction between the uncreated God and the created order' (*Oxford Dictionary of the Christian Church*, third edition, Oxford University Press, 1997, p. 1104).
[83] *Modernist*, name given those who at the beginning of the twentieth century tried to reconcile traditional catholic teaching with the latest scientific discoveries but ended up, in Teilhard's view, by diminishing the person of Christ. Teilhard was no modernist. 'The modernist "volatilizes" Christ and dissolves him in the world. While I am trying to concentrate the world in Christ' (Teilhard, Cahier 7, 9 June 1919, in Bruno de Solages, *Teilhard de Chardin*, Privat, 1967, p. 342).
[84] *Illuminati*, name given to several bodies of religious enthusiasts such as the sixteenth-century Alumbrados or the Rosicrucians (*Oxford Dictionary of the Christian Church*, p. 820).
[85] S. Angela of Foligno (*c.*1248–1309), *Le Livre des visions et instructions* (Seuil, 1991, p. 73)..

and verifiable truth of the Gospel event. The Mystical Christ, the Universal Christ of S. Paul, has neither meaning nor value in our eyes except as an expansion of the Christ who was born of Mary and who died on the Cross. The former essentially draws his fundamental quality of undeniability and concreteness from the latter. However far we may be drawn into the divine spaces opened up to us by christian mysticism, we never depart from the Jesus of the Gospels. On the contrary, we feel a growing need to enfold ourselves ever more firmly within his human truth. We are not, therefore, modernist in the condemned sense of the word. Nor shall we end up among the visionaries and the 'illuminati'.

The real error of the visionaries is to confuse the different planes of the world, and consequently to mix up their activities. In the view of the 'illuminati', the divine presence illuminates not only the heart of things, but tends to invade their surface and therefore do away with their exacting but salutary reality. The gradual maturing of immediate causes, the complicated network of material deter-minisms, the infinite susceptibilities of the universal order, no longer count. But through this seamless veil and these delicate threads, divine action is imagined as appearing naked and without order. And then the falsely miraculous comes to disconcert and obstruct the human effort.

As we have already abundantly shown, the effect produced upon human activity by the true transformation of the world in Jesus Christ is utterly different. At the heart of the divine milieu, as the Church reveals it, things are transfigured, but from within. They bathe interiorly in light, but, in this incandescence, they retain—this is not strong enough, they exalt—all that is most specific in their attributes. We can only lose ourselves in God by prolonging the most individual characteristics of beings far beyond themselves: that is the fundamental rule by which we can always distinguish true mystics from their counterfeits. The heart of God is boundless, *'multæ mansiones'* ('many mansions').[86] And yet in all that immensity there is only one possible place for each one of us at any given moment, the one we are led to by unflagging fidelity to the natural and supernatural duties of life. At this point, which we can reach at the right moment only if we exert the maximum effort on every plane, God will reveal himself in all his plenitude. Except at this point, the divine milieu, although it may still enfold us, exists only incompletely, or not at all, for us. Thus its great waters do not call us to defeat but to constant struggle to stem their flow. Their energy awaits and provokes our energy. Just as on certain days the sea lights up only as the ship's prow or the swimmer cleaves its surface, so the world is only lit up with God when it reacts to our impulse. When God desires ultimately to subject and unite christians to him, by ecstasy or by death, it is as though he bears them away stiffened by love and by obedience in the full extent of their effort.

It might look from now on as though believers in the divine milieu were falling back into the errors of a pagan naturalism in reaction to the excesses of quietism and illuminism. With their faith in the heavenly value of human effort, by their expectation of a new awakening of the faculties of adoration dormant in the world, by their respect for the spiritual powers still latent in matter, christians may often bear a striking resemblance to the worshippers of the earth.

But here again, as in the case of pantheism, the resemblance is only external and such as is so often found in opposite things.

Pagans love the earth to enjoy it and to confine themselves within it; christians to make it purer and to draw strength from it, in order to escape from it.

Pagans seek to espouse sensible things to extract delight from them; they adhere to the world. Christians multiply their contacts with the world only to harness, or submit to, the energies which they will take back, or which will take them, to heaven. They pre-adhere to God.

Pagans think that human beings divinize themselves by closing in on themselves; the final act of human evolution is when individuals or the whole constitute themselves within themselves. Christians

---

[86] *'In domo Patris mei mansiones multæ sunt'* ['In My Father's house are many mansions'] (Jn 14.2 NKJ).

only see their divinization in the assimilation of their achievement through an 'Other': the culmination of life, in their eyes, is death in union.

For pagans, universal reality only exists in its projection onto the plane of the tangible: it is immediate and multiple. Christians take exactly the same elements: but they prolong them along their common axis which links them to God; and, by the same token, the universe is unified for them, although it is only attainable at the final center of its consummation.

To sum up, we can say that, compared to all the main historical forms assumed by the human religious spirit, christian mysticism extracts all that is sweetest and strongest circulating in all the human mysticisms, without absorbing their evil or suspect elements. It shows an astonishing equilibrium between the active and the passive, between possession of the world and its renunciation, between a taste for things and an indifference to them. Why should we be astonished by this shifting harmony? Is it not the natural and spontaneous reaction of the soul to the stimulus of a milieu which is exactly, by nature and grace, the one in which that soul is made to live and develop itself? Just as, at the center of the divine milieu, all the sounds of created being are fused, without being confused, in a single note which dominates and sustains them (that seraphic note, no doubt, which bewitched S. Francis), so all the powers of the soul begin to resound in response to its call; and these multiple tones, in their turn, compose themselves into a single, ineffably simple vibration in which all the spiritual nuances—of love and intellect, of ardor and calm, of fullness and ecstasy, of passion and indifference, of assimilation and surrender, of rest and movement—are born, pass and shine forth, according to time and circumstance, like the countless possibilities of an interior attitude, inexpressible and unique.

And if any words could translate that permanent and lucid intoxication better than others, perhaps they would be 'passionate indifference'.

To have access to the divine milieu is to have found the unique necessary being, that is, the one who burns by enflaming everything that we would love badly or insufficiently; the one who calms by eclipsing with his flames everything that we would love too much; the one who consoles by gathering up everything that has been torn away from our love or has never been given to it. To reach these priceless layers is to experience, with equal truth, that we have need of everything, and that we have need of nothing. We have need of everything because the world will never be large enough to provide our zest for action with the means of grasping God, or our thirst for undergoing with the possibility of being invaded by him. And yet we have need of nothing: because the only reality which can satisfy us lies beyond the transparencies in which it is mirrored, everything that fades away and dies between us will only serve to give back reality to us with greater purity. Everything means both everything and nothing to me; everything is God to me and everything is dust to me: that is what we can say with equal truth, in accord with how the divine ray falls.

'Which do you think is the greater of two beatitudes,' someone once asked, 'to have the sublime unity of God to center and save the universe? Or to have the concrete immensity of the universe by which to undergo and touch God?'

We shall not seek to escape this joyful uncertainty. But now that we are familiar with the attributes of the divine milieu, we shall turn our attention to the Thing itself which appeared to us in the depth of each being, like a radiant countenance, like a fascinating abyss. And now we can ask him, 'Who are you, Lord?'[87]

2

Nature of the divine milieu
The Universal Christ and the great communion

We can say as a first approximation that the milieu whose rich and mobile homogeneity has revealed itself all around us like a condition

---

[87] '*Quis es Domine?*' (Acts 9.5).

and a consequence of the most christian attitudes (such as right intention and resignation) is formed by the divine omnipresence. The immensity of God is the essential attribute which allows us to seize him universally within and around us.

This answer begins to satisfy our minds because it circumscribes the problem. However, it does not yet give the power *'in qua vivimus et sumus'* ('in whom we live and have our being')[88] the sharp lines with which we should wish to trace the features of the unique necessary being. Under what form, proper to our creation and adapted to our universe, does the divine immensity manifest itself to—and become relevant to—humanity? We feel it charged with that sanctifying grace which the catholic faith causes to circulate everywhere as the true sap of the world; which, in its attributes, is very like that charity, *'manete in dilectione mea'* ('Abide in my love'),[89] which one day, the Scriptures tell us, will be the unique stable principle of natures and powers; be the only stable principle of natures and powers; which, too, is fundamentally similar to the wonderful and substantial divine will, whose marrow is everywhere present and constitutes the true food of our lives, *'omne delectamentum in se habentem'* ('Filled with all sweetness and delight').[90] What, in the end, is the concrete link which binds all these universal entities together and confers on them a final power of gaining hold of us?

The essence of christianity consists in asking ourselves this question, and in answering: 'The Word Incarnate, our Lord Jesus Christ.'

Let us examine step by step how we can validate in our eyes this prodigious identification of the Son of Man and the divine milieu.

A first step, unquestionably, is to see the divine omnipresence in which we find ourselves plunged as an omnipresence of action. God enfolds us and penetrates us by creating and preserving us.

---

[88] The Vulgate reads: *'In ipso enim vivimus et movemur et sumus'* ['In him we live and move and have our being'] (Acts 17.28).

[89] Jn 15.9.

[90] Response from the *Parvum Officium Sanctissimi Sacramenti*—Little Office of the Blessed Sacrament, traditionally recited on Thursdays in commemoration of the Last Supper.

Now let us go a little further. Under what form, and with what end in view, has the Creator given us, and still preserves in us, the gift of participated being? Under the form of an essential aspiration towards him—and with a view to the unhoped-for adhesion which is to make us one and the same complex thing with him. The action by which God maintains us in the field of his presence is a unitive transformation.

Let us go further still. What is the supreme and complex reality for which the divine operation molds us? It is revealed to us by S. Paul and S. John. It is the quantitative repletion and the qualitative consummation of all things: it is the mysterious Pleroma, in which the substantial one and the created multiple fuse without confusion in a whole which, without adding anything essential to God, will nevertheless be a kind of triumph and generalization of being.

At last we are nearing our goal. What is the active center, the living link, the organizing soul of the Pleroma? S. Paul, again, proclaims it with all his power: it is he in whom everything is reunited, and in whom all things are consummated—through whom the whole created edifice receives its consistency—Christ dead and risen *'qui replet omnia'* ('who fills all things'),[91] *'in quo omnia constant'* ('in whom all things consist').[92]

And now let us link the first and last terms of this long series of identities. We shall then see with a wave of joy that the divine omnipresence translates itself within our universe by the network of the organizing forces of the total Christ. God exerts pressure, in us and upon us—through the intermediary of all the powers of heaven, earth and hell—only in the act of forming and consummating Christ who saves and super-animates the world. And since, in the course of this operation, Christ himself does not act as a dead or passive point of convergence, but as a center of radiation for the energies which lead the universe back to God through his humanity, the layers of divine action finally come to us impregnated with his organic energies.

[91] Cf. Col 2.10.
[92] Cf. Col 1.17.

From now on the divine milieu assumes for us the savor and the specific features which we desire. We recognize in it an omnipresence which acts upon us by assimilating us to itself, *'in unitate Corporis Christi'* ('in the unity of the Body of Christ'). The divine immensity, as a consequence of the Incarnation, is transformed for us into the omnipresence of christification. All the good that I can do *'opus et operatio'* is physically gathered in, by something of itself, into the reality of the consummated Christ. All that I endure, with faith and love, of diminishment and death, makes me a little more closely integrated part of his Mystical Body. This is exactly the Christ whom we make or whom we undergo in all things. Not only *'diligentibus omnia convertuntur in bonum'* ('all things are transformed into good') but, more clearly still, *'convertuntur in Deum'* ('transformed into God') and, quite explicitly, *'convertuntur in Christum'* ('transformed into Christ').

Despite the strength of S. Paul's expressions (formulated, we should not forget, for ordinary men and women among the first christians) some readers may feel that we have been led to strain, in too realist a direction, the notion of the Mystical Body—or at least that we have allowed ourselves to seek esoteric perspectives in it. But if we look a little more closely, we shall see that we have simply taken another path to rejoin the great highway opened up in the Church by the onrush of the cult of the Holy Eucharist.

When the priest says the words *'Hoc est Corpus meum'* ('This is my Body'),[93] his words fall directly on to the bread and directly transform it into the individual reality of Christ. But the great sacramental operation does not cease at that local and momentary event. Even children are taught that—throughout the life of each one of us, and the life of the Church, and the history of the world—there is only one Mass and only one Communion. Christ died once in agony. Peter and Paul receive communion on such and such a day at a particular hour. But these different acts are only the diversely central points in which the continuity of a unique act is

---

[93] Cf. Mt 26.26; Mk 14.22; Lk 22.19; 1 Cor 11.24. Words of consecration in the Eucharist.

split up and fixed, in space and time, for our experience. In fact, from the beginning of the messianic preparation until the Parousia, passing through the historic manifestation of Jesus and the phases of growth of his Church, a single event has been developing in the world: the Incarnation, realized, in each individual, through the Eucharist.

All the communions of a lifetime are one communion.

All the communions of all those now living are one communion.

All the communions of all those, past, present and future, are one communion.

Have we ever sufficiently considered the physical immensity of human beings, and their extraordinary relations with the universe, to realize in our minds the formidable implications of this elementary truth?

Let us imagine in our minds, as best we can, the vast multitudes of men and women in every epoch and in every land. According to the catechism we believe that this fearful anonymous throng is, by right, subject to the physical and overmastering contact of the one whose appanage it is to be able *'omnia sibi subicere'* ('subject all things to himself')[94] (by right, and to a certain extent in fact; for who can tell where the diffusion of Christ, with the influence of grace, stops, as it spreads outwards from the faithful at the heart of the human family?). Yes, the human layer of the earth is wholly and continuously under the organizing influx of the Incarnate Christ. This we all believe, as one of the most certain points of our faith.

Now how does the human world itself appear within the structure of the universe? We have already spoken about this,[95] and the more we think about it the more we are struck by the obviousness and importance of the following conclusion: it appears as a zone of continuous spiritual transformation, where all inferior realities and forces without exception are sublimated into sensations, feelings, ideas, and the powers of knowledge and love. Around the earth, the

---

[94] The Vulgate reads: *'subicere sibi omnia'* ['all things subject to himself'] (Phil 3.21).
[95] See above under 'The divinization of our activities—the definitive solution'.

center of our field of vision, our souls form, in some way, the incandescent surface of matter plunged in God. From the dynamic and biological point of view it is quite as impossible to draw a line below it, as to draw a line between a plant and the environment that sustains it. If, then, the Eucharist is a sovereign influence upon our human natures, then its energy necessarily extends, owing to the effects of continuity, into the less luminous regions that sustain us; *'descendit ad inferos'*,[96] we might say. At every moment the Eucharistic Christ controls, from the point of view of the organization of the Pleroma (which is the only true point of view from which the world can be understood), the whole movement of the universe,—Christ *'per quem omnia, Domine, semper creas, vivificas et præstas nobis'* ('through all things, Lord, ever creating, reviving and anticipating us').

The control we are speaking of is, at the minimum, a final refinement, a final purification, a final harnessing, of all the elements which can be used in the construction of the New Earth. But how can we avoid going further and believing that the sacramental action of Christ, precisely because it sanctifies matter, extends its influence beyond the pure supernatural, over all that makes up the internal and external ambience of the faithful, that is, that it sets its mark in everything which we call 'our providence'?

If this is the case, then we find ourselves (by simply having followed the 'extensions' of the Eucharist) plunged once again precisely into our divine milieu. Christ—for whom and in whom we are formed, each with our own individuality and our own vocation—reveals himself in each reality around us, and shines like an ultimate determinant, like a center, we might almost say like a universal element. As our humanity assimilates the material world, and as the Host assimilates our humanity, the eucharistic transformation goes beyond and completes the transubstantiation of the bread on the altar. Step by step it irresistibly invades the universe. It is the fire that sweeps over the heath; the stroke that vibrates through the bronze.

---

[96] A possible play on the words of the Apostles' Creed (*Symbolum Apostolorum*): *'descendit ad infernos'* ['he descended to hell'].

In a secondary and generalized sense, but in a true sense, the sacramental species are formed by the totality of the world, and the duration of creation is the time needed for its consecration. *'In Christo vivimus, movemur et sumus'* ('In Christ we live and move and have our being).[97]

Grant, O God, that when I draw near to the altar to communicate, I may discern from now on the infinite perspectives hidden beneath the smallness and the nearness of the Host in which you are concealed. I have already accustomed myself to seeing, beneath the stillness of that piece of bread, a devouring power which, in the words of your greatest Doctors, far from being consumed by me, consumes me. Give me the strength to rise above the remaining illusions which tend to make me think of your touch as circumscribed and momentary.

I am beginning to understand: under the sacramental species it is primarily through the 'accidents' of matter that you touch me, but, as a consequence, it is also through the whole universe to the extent that this ebbs and flows over me under your primary influence. In a true sense the arms and the heart which you open to me are nothing less than all the united powers of the world which, penetrated and permeated to their depths by your will, your tastes and your temperament, converge upon my being to form it, nourish it and bear it along towards the center of your fire. In the Host it is my life that you are offering me, O Jesus.

What can I do to gather up and answer that universal and enveloping embrace? 'Quomodo comprehendam ut comprehensus sum?' ('How can I understand what holds me captive?')[98] *To the total offer that is made me, I can only answer by a total acceptance. I shall therefore react to the eucharistic contact with the entire effort of my life—of my life today and of my life of tomorrow, of my personal life and of my life as linked to all other lives. Periodically, the sacred species may perhaps fade away in me. But every time they will leave me a little more deeply engulfed in the layers of your omnipresence: living and dying, I shall never at any moment cease to move forwards in you. Thus the precept implicit in your Church, that we must communicate everywhere and always, is justified*

---

[97] The Vulgate reads: *'in ipso enim vivimus et movemur et sumus'* (Acts 17.28).

[98] Cf. the Vulgate: *'Non quod iam acceperim aut iam perfectus sim sequor autem si conprehendam in quo et conprehensus sum a Christo Iesu'* ['Not that I have already attained, or am already perfected;

with extraordinary force and precision. The Eucharist must invade my life. My life must become, as a result of the sacrament, an unlimited and endless contact with you—that life which seemed, a few moments ago, like a baptism with you in the waters of the world, now reveals itself to me as communion with you through the world. It is the sacrament of life. The sacrament of my life—of my life received, of my life lived, of my life surrendered . . .

Because you ascended into heaven after having descended into hell, you have so filled the universe in every direction, Jesus, that from now on it is blessedly impossible for us to escape you. 'Quo ibo ab spiritu tuo et quo a facie tua fugiam' *('Where can I go from your spirit ? Or where can I flee from your presence?').*[99] *Now I know that for certain. Neither life, whose advance increases your hold upon me; nor death, which throws me into your hands; nor the good or evil spiritual powers which are your living instruments; nor the energies of matter into which you are plunged; nor the irreversible stream of duration whose rhythm and flow you control without appeal; nor the unfathomable abysses of space which are the measure of your greatness;* neque mors, neque vita, neque angeli, neque principatus, neque potestates, neque virtutes, neque instantia, neque futura, neque fortitudo, neque altitudo, neque profundum, neque creatura alia (*'neither death, nor life, nor angels, nor rulers, nor things present, nor things to come, nor powers, nor height, nor depth, nor anything else in all creation'*)[100]—*none of these things will be able to separate me from your substantial love, because they are all only the veil, the 'species', under which you take hold of me in order that I may take hold of you.*

Once again, Lord, I ask which is the most precious of these two beatitudes: that all things for me should be a contact with you? or that you should be so 'universal' that I can undergo you and grasp you in every creature?

Sometimes people think that they can increase your attraction in my eyes by stressing almost exclusively the charm and goodness of your human life in the past. But truly, O Lord, if I wanted to cherish only a human, then I would surely turn

---

but I press on, that I may lay hold of that for which Christ Jesus has also laid hold of me] (Phil 3.12 NKJ).

[99] Ps 138.7 (Vulgate). Ps 138.7 in the Vulgate is Ps 139.7 in modern translations.

[100] Teilhard is quoting here from memory: cf. Rom 8.38–39.

to those whom you have given me in the allurement of their present flowering. Are there not, with our mothers, brothers, sisters and friends, enough irresistibly lovable people around us? Why should we turn to the Judæa of two thousand years ago? No, what I cry out for, like every being, with my whole life and with all my earthly passion, is something very different from an equal to cherish: it is a God to adore.

To adore, that is, to lose ourselves in the unfathomable, to plunge into the inexhaustible, to find peace in the incorruptible, to be absorbed in defined immensity, to offer ourselves to the fire and the transparency, to annihilate ourselves as we become more deliberately conscious of ourselves, and to give of our deepest to that whose depth has no end. Whom, then, can we adore?

The more humans become human, the more they will become prey to a need, a need that is always more explicit, more subtle and more magnificent, the need to adore.

Disperse, O Jesus, the clouds with your lightning! Show yourself to us as the Mighty, the Radiant, the Risen! Come to us once again as the Pantocrator who filled the solitude of the cupolas in the ancient basilicas! Nothing less than this Parousia is needed to counter-balance and dominate in our hearts the glory of the world that is coming into view. And so that we should triumph over the world with you, come to us clothed in the glory of the world.

3
Growth of the divine milieu

The Kingdom of God is within us. When Christ appears in the clouds he will simply be manifesting a metamorphosis that has been slowly accomplished under his influence in the heart of the mass of humanity. To hasten his coming, let us therefore concentrate upon a better understanding of the process by which the Holy Presence is born and grows within us. To foster its progress more intelligently let us observe the birth and growth of the divine milieu, first in ourselves and then in the world that begins with us.

The Divine Milieu

A. *The coming of the divine milieu. The taste for being and the diaphany of God*

A breeze passes in the night. When did it spring up? Where does it come from? Where is it going? No one knows. No one can compel the spirit, the gaze or the light of God to descend upon them.

On some given day they suddenly become conscious that they are alive to a particular perception of the divine spread everywhere about them. Question them. When did this state begin for them? They cannot tell. All they know is that a new spirit has crossed their lives.

'It began with a particular and unique resonance which swelled each harmony, with a diffused radiance which haloed each beauty . . . All the elements of psychological life were in turn affected; sensations, feelings, thoughts. Every day they became more fragrant, more colored, more intense by means of an indefinable thing—always the same thing. Then the vague note, fragrance, and light began to define themselves. And then, contrary to all expectation and all probability, I began to feel what was ineffably common to all things. The unity communicated itself to me by giving me the gift of grasping it. I had in fact acquired a new sense, the sense of a new quality or a new dimension. Deeper still: a transformation had taken place for me in the very perception of being. From now on being had become, in some way, tangible and savorous to me. And as it came to dominate all the forms which it assumed, being itself began to draw me and to intoxicate me.'

That is what anyone might say, more or less explicitly, who has gone any distance in the development of their capacity for self-analysis. Outwardly they could well be pagans. And if they happen to be christians, they would admit that this interior reversal seemed to them to have occurred within the profane and 'natural' parts of their souls.

But we must not allow ourselves to be deceived by appearances. We must not let ourselves be disconcerted by the patent errors into which many mystics have fallen in their attempts to place or even to name the universal smile. As with all power (and the richer, the more

91

so) the sense of the All comes to birth rudimentary and troubled. It often happens that, like children opening their eyes for the first time, men and women do not accurately place the reality which they sense behind things. Their gropings often meet with nothing but a metaphysical phantom or a crude idol. But images and reflections have never proved anything against the reality of objects and the light. The false trails of pantheism bear witness to our immense need for some revealing word to come from the mouth of the one who is. With that reservation, it remains true that, physiologically, the so-called 'natural' taste for being is, in each life, the first dawn of the divine illumination—the first tremor perceived of the world animated by the Incarnation. The sense (which is not necessarily the feeling) of the omnipresence of God prolongs, super-creates and supernaturalizes the identical physiological energy which, in a mutilated or misdirected form, produces the various pantheisms.[101]

Once we realize that the divine milieu discloses itself to us as a modification of the deep being of things, it is at once possible to make two important observations touching the manner in which its perception is introduced and preserved within our human perspectives.

In the first place, the manifestation of the divine no more modifies the apparent order of things than the eucharistic consecration modifies the sacred species to our eyes. Since the psychological event consists, at first, solely in the appearance of an interior tension or deep brilliance, the relations between creatures remain exactly the same. They are merely accentuated in meaning. Like those translucent materials which a light within them can illuminate as a whole, the world appears to christian mystics bathed in an interior light which intensifies its relief, its structure and its depths. This light is

---

[101] In other words and more simply: just as in the love of God (charity) can be found, quite obviously, the human power to love in its supernatural state—so, in the same way, we believe that at the psychological origin of the 'feeling of omnipresence', experienced by christians, can be found 'the sense of universal being' which is the source of most human mysticisms. There is a soul which is *naturaliter christiana*. It should be remembered (cf. *Introduction*) that these pages contain a psychological description, not a theological explanation, of the states of soul encountered. (Author's Note.)

not the superficial glimmer which can be realized in coarse enjoyment. Nor is it the violent flash which destroys objects and blinds our eyes. It is the calm and powerful radiance engendered by the synthesis of all the elements of the world in Jesus. The more fulfilled, according to their nature, are the beings in whom it comes to play, the closer and more sensible this radiance appears; and the more sensible it becomes, the more objects which it bathes become distinct in contour and remote in substance. If we may slightly alter a hallowed expression, we could say that the great mystery of christianity is not exactly the appearance, but the transparence, of God in the universe. *Yes, Lord, not only the ray that strikes the surface, but the ray that penetrates. Not only your Epiphany, Jesus, but your Diaphany.*

Nothing is more consistent or more fleeting—more fused with things or at the same time more separable from them—than a ray of light. If the divine milieu reveals itself to us as an incandescence of the interior layers of being, who is to guarantee us the persistence of this vision? No one other than the ray of light itself. The Diaphany whose joys no power in the world can prevent us from savoring because it occurs at a level deeper than any power; and no power in the world, for the same reason, can compel its appearance.

That is the second point, the consideration of which should be used as the basis for all our further reflections on the progress of life in God.

The perception of the divine omnipresence is essentially a seeing, a taste, that is, a kind of intuition bearing upon certain superior qualities in things. It cannot, therefore, be attained directly by any process of reasoning, nor by any human artifice. It is a gift, like life itself, of which it is undoubtedly the supreme experiential perfection. And so we are brought back again to the center of ourselves, to the edge of that mysterious source to which we descended (at the beginning of Part Two) and watched it as it welled up. To experience the attraction of God, to be sensible of the beauty, the consistency and the final unity of being, is the highest and at the same time the most complete of our 'passivities of growth'. God tends, by the logic of his creative effort, to make himself sought and perceived by us:

'*Posuit homines . . . si forte attrectent eum*' ('he has appointed human beings . . . so strongly do they relate to him'). His prevenient grace is therefore always on the alert to excite our first look and our first prayer. But in the end the initiative, the awakening, always come from him, and whatever the further developments of our mystical faculties, no progress is achieved in this domain except as the new response to a new gift. '*Nemo venit ad me, nisi Pater traxerit eum*' ('no one comes to me unless drawn by the Father who sent me').[102]

We are thus led to posit intense and continual prayer at the origin of our invasion by the divine milieu, the prayer which begs for the fundamental gift: '*Domine, fac ut videam*' ('Lord, let me see again').[103] *Lord, we know and feel that you are everywhere around us. But it seems that there is a veil before our eyes.* 'Illumina vultum tuum super nos' ('*Make your face to shine upon us*').[104] *Let the light of your countenance shine upon us in its universality.* 'Sit splendor Domini nostri super nos' ('*Let the brightness of our God be upon us*').[105] *Let your deep brilliance light up the innermost parts of the massive obscurities in which we move. And, to that end, send us your spirit,* 'Spiritus principalis' ('*the ruling (or presiding) spirit*'), *whose flaming action alone can operate the birth and achievement of the great metamorphosis which sums up all interior perfection and towards which your creation yearns:* 'Emitte Spiritum tuum, et creabuntur et renovabis faciem terræ' ('*You send forth your spirit, they are created; and you renew the face of the earth*').[106]

B. *Individual progress in the divine milieu: purity, faith and fidelity—the operatives*

'*Ego operor . . . Pater semper operatur*' ('I am working . . . My Father is always working').[107] The delight of the divine milieu (heavy with

---

[102] Cf. Jn 6.44.

[103] Cf. Lk 18.41.

[104] Cf. Ps 66.2 (Vulgate). Ps 66.2 in the Vulgate is Ps 67.1 in modern translations.

[105] Ps 89.17 (Vulgate) actually reads: '*sit splendor Domini Dei nostri super nos*' ['Let the brightness of the Lord our God be upon us'] (Ps 90.17 NKJ).

[106] Ps 103.30 (Vulgate). Ps 103.30 in the Vulgate is Ps 104.30 in modern translations.

responsibilities) is that it can assume an ever-increasing intensity around us. We could say that it is an atmosphere ever more luminous and ever more charged with God. It is in him and in him alone that the reckless vow of all love is realized: to lose ourselves in what we love, to sink ourselves in it more and more.

It could be said that three virtues contribute with particular effectiveness towards the limitless concentration of the divine in our lives—purity, faith, and fidelity; three virtues which appear to be 'static' but which are in fact the three most active and unconfined virtues of all. Let us look at them one after the other and examine their generative function in the divine milieu.

1. Purity

Purity, in the wide sense of the word, is not merely abstaining from wrong (that is only a negative aspect of purity), nor even chastity (which is only a remarkable special instance of it). It is the rectitude and the impulse introduced into our lives by the love of God sought in and above everything.

They are spiritually impure who, lingering in pleasure or shut up in selfishness, introduce, within themselves and around themselves, a principle of slowing-down and division in the unification of the universe in God.

They are pure, on the other hand, who, in accord with their place in the world, seek to give Christ's desire to consummate all things precedence over their own immediate and momentary advantage.

Still purer and more pure are those who, attracted by God, succeed in giving that movement and impulse an ever greater continuity, intensity, and reality—whether their vocation calls them to move always in the material zones of the world (though more and more spiritually), or whether, as is more often the case, they have access to regions where the divine gradually replaces for them all other earthly nourishment.

---

[107] The Vulgate reads: *'Iesus autem respondit eis Pater meus usque modo operatur et ego operor'* ['My Father is still working, and I also am working'] (Jn 5.17).

Thus understood, the purity of beings is measured by the degree of the attraction that draws them towards the divine center, or, what comes to the same thing, by their proximity to the center. Christian experience teaches us that it is preserved by recollection, mental prayer, purity of conscience, purity of intention, and the sacraments. Let us be satisfied, here, with extolling its wonderful power of condensing the divine in all around us.

In one of his stories, Robert Hugh Benson[108] tells of a 'visionary' coming upon a lonely chapel where a nun is praying. He enters. All at once he sees the whole world bound up and moving and organizing itself around that remote spot, in tune with the intensity and inflection of the desires of that puny, praying figure. The convent chapel had become the axis about which the earth revolved. The contemplative sensitized and animated all things because she believed; and her faith was operative because her very pure soul placed her near to God. This piece of fiction is an admirable parable.

The interior tension of the mind towards God may seem negligible to those who try to calculate the quantity of energy accumulated in the mass of humanity.

And yet, if we could see the 'light invisible' as we can see clouds or lightning or the rays of the sun, a pure soul would seem as active in this world, by virtue of its sheer purity, as the snowy summits whose impassable peaks breathe in continually for us the roving powers of the high atmosphere.

Do we want the divine milieu to grow all around us? Let us jealously guard and nourish all the forces of union, of desire, and of prayer that grace offers us. By the mere fact that our transparency will increase, the divine light, that never ceases to press in upon us, will irrupt more powerfully.

Have we ever thought of the meaning of the mystery of the Annunciation?

When the time had come when God resolved to realize his Incarnation before our eyes, he had first of all to raise up in the world

---

[108] Robert Hugh Benson (1871–1914), catholic convert, author and apologist.

a virtue capable of drawing him as far as ourselves. He needed a mother who would engender him in the human sphere. What did he do? He created the Virgin Mary, that is, he called forth on earth a purity so great that, within this transparency, he would concentrate himself to the point of appearing as a little child.

Thus, expressed in its strength and reality, is the power of purity to bring the divine to birth among us.

And yet the Church, addressing the Virgin Mother, adds: *'Beata quæ credidisti'* ('blessed is she who believed').[109] For it is in faith that purity finds the fulfillment of its fertility.

2. Faith

Faith, as we understand it here, is not, of course, simply the intellectual adherence to christian dogma. It is taken in a much richer sense to mean belief in God charged with all the trust in his beneficent strength that knowledge of the divine being arouses in us. It means the practical conviction that the universe, between the hands of the Creator, continues to be the clay in which he shapes innumerable possibilities according to his will. In a word, it is evangelical faith, of which it can be said that no virtue, not even charity, was more strongly urged by the Savior.

Now, under what guise was this disposition so untiringly revealed to us by the words and deeds of the master? Above all and beyond all as an operative power. But, intimidated by the assertions of an unproven positivism, or put off by the mystical excesses of 'Christian Science',[110] we are sometimes tempted to gloss over the disconcerting promise that the efficacy of prayer is tangible and certain. Yet we cannot ignore it without blushing for Christ. If we do not believe, the waves engulf us, the winds blow, nourishment fails, sickness lays us low or kills us, the divine power is impotent or remote. If, on the other hand, we believe, the waters are welcoming and sweet, the bread is multiplied, our eyes opened, the dead rise

---

[109] Lk 1.45.

[110] *Christian Science*, system founded by Mary Baker Eddy (1821–1910) known chiefly for

again, the power of God is, as it were, drawn from him by force and spreads throughout all nature. We must either arbitrarily minimize or explain away the Gospels, or we must admit the reality of these effects, not as transient and past, but as perennial and true at this moment. Let us beware of stifling this revelation of a possible vitalization of the forces of nature in God. Let us, rather, place it resolutely at the center of our vision of the world—careful, only, that we understand it right.

Faith is operative. What does this mean? Is divine action, at the call of faith, going to replace the normal interplay of the causes which surround us? Do we, like the 'illuminati' of old, expect God to bring about directly, upon matter or upon our bodies, results that have hitherto been obtained by our own industrious research?

Obviously not. Neither the interior inter-relations of the material or psychical world, nor our duty to make the greatest possible effort, are in any way undermined, or even relaxed, by the precepts of faith. *'Iota unum aut unus apex non præteribit'* ('Not an iota, not a dot, will pass').[111] All the natural links of the world remain intact under the transforming action of 'operative faith'; but a principle, an interior finality, we might almost say an additional soul, is superimposed upon them. Under the influence of our faith, the universe is capable, without outwardly changing its characteristics, of becoming more supple, more fully animated—of becoming 'super-animated'. This is the 'at the most' and the 'at the least' of the belief expressly imposed upon us by the Gospels. Sometimes this 'super-animation' expresses itself in miraculous effects—when the transfiguration of causes permits them access to the zone of their 'obediential potency'. At other times, and this is the more usual case, it is manifested by the integration of unimportant or unfavorable events within a higher plane and within a higher providence.

We have already mentioned and analyzed a very typical example

its concern with healing through prayer alone. 'Evil and sickness have no ultimate reality and are to be destroyed by the subject's becoming aware of God's power and love (rather than by medical treatment).' (*Oxford Dictionary of the Christian Church*, p. 334.)
[111] Mt 5.18 (Revised Standard).

of this second form of divinization of the world by faith (a form no less profound and no less precious than more striking prodigies). In considering the passivities of diminishment we saw how our failures, our death, our faults even, could, through God, be recast into something better and transformed in him. The moment has come to envisage this miracle in its most general sense and from the particular point of view of the act of faith which is, on our part, its providential condition.

In our hands, in the hands of all of us, the world and life (our world, our life) are placed like a Host, ready to be charged with the divine influence, that is, with a real presence of the Incarnate Word. The mystery will be accomplished. But on one condition: which is that we shall believe that this has the will and the power to become for us the action, that is, the prolongation of the Body of Christ. Do we believe? If we do, everything is illuminated and takes shape around us: chance is seen to be order, success assumes an incorruptible plenitude, suffering becomes a visit and a caress of God. Do we hesitate? If we do, the rock remains dry, the sky dark, the waters treacherous and shifting. And we may hear the voice of the master, faced with our bungled lives: 'You of little faith, why did you doubt?'[112]

'Domine, adjuva incredulitatem meam' (*Lord, help my unbelief*).[113] *Ah, you know it yourself, Lord, through having humanly borne its anguish: on certain days the world seems a terrifying thing: huge, blind and brutal. It buffets us about, drags us along, and kills us with complete indifference. Heroically, it may truly be said, we have contrived to create a more or less habitable zone of light and warmth in the midst of the great, cold, black waters—a zone where people have eyes to see, hands to help, and hearts to love. But how precarious that habitation is! At any moment the vast and horrible thing may break in through the cracks—the thing which we try hard to forget is always there, separated from us by a flimsy partition: fire, pestilence, storms, earthquakes, or the unleashing of dark moral forces—these callously sweep away in*

---

[112] Mt 14.31.
[113] Cf. Mk 9.23 (Vulgate). Mk 9.23 (Vulgate) is Mk 9.24 in modern translations.

one moment what we had laboriously built up and beautified with all our intelligence and all our love.

Since my human dignity, O God, forbids me to close my eyes to this, like an animal or a child—that I may not succumb to the temptation to curse the universe and the one who made it—teach me to adore it by seeing you concealed within it. O Lord, repeat to me the great liberating words, the words which at once reveal and operate: 'Hoc est Corpus meum' (*'This is my body'*).[114] *Truly, the huge and dark thing, the phantom, the tempest—if we want it to be so, is you!* 'Ego sum nolite timere' (*'It is I; do not be afraid'*).[115] *The things in our lives which terrify us, the things which threw you yourself into agony in the Garden, are, ultimately, only the species or appearance, the matter of one and the same sacrament.*

We have only to believe. And the more threatening and irreducible reality appears, the more firmly and desperately must we believe. Then, little by little, we shall see the universal horror unbend, and then smile upon us and take us in its more than human arms.

No, it is not the rigid determinism of matter and large numbers, but the subtle combinations of spirit, that give the universe its consistency. The immense hazard and the immense blindness of the world are only an illusion to those who believe. *'Fides, substantia rerum'* ('Faith is the substance of things').[116]

3. Fidelity

Because we have believed intensely and with a pure heart in the world, the world will open the arms of God to us. It is for us to throw ourselves into these arms so that the circle of the divine milieu may close round our lives. That gesture of ours will be one of an active response to our daily task. Faith consecrates the world. Fidelity communicates with it.

To give a worthy description of the 'advantages' of fidelity, that

---

[114] Mt 26.26; Mk 14.22; Lk 22.19; 1 Cor 11.24. Words of consecration in the Eucharist.
[115] Mt 14.27.
[116] Heb 11.1 (NKJ).

100

is, of the essential and final role which it plays in our taking possession of the divine milieu, we should have to go back to what was said in the first two parts of this study. For it is fidelity which releases the inexhaustible resources offered by every 'passion' to our desire for communion.

Through fidelity we situate ourselves and maintain ourselves in the divine hands so exactly as to become one with them in their action.

Through fidelity we open ourselves so intimately and continuously to the wishes and good pleasure of God, that his life penetrates and assimilates ours like a fortifying bread. *'Hoc est cibus meus, ut faciam voluntatem Patris'* ('My food is to do the will of the Father').[117]

Through fidelity, finally, we find ourselves at every moment situated at the exact point at which the whole bundle of the interior and exterior forces of the world converge providentially upon us, that is, at the point where the divine milieu can, at a given moment, be made real for us.

It is fidelity, and fidelity alone, that enables us to welcome the universal and perpetual overtures of the divine milieu; through fidelity, and fidelity alone, can we return to God the kiss he is for ever offering us across the world.

What is without price in the 'communicating' power of fidelity is that, like the power possessed by faith and purity, it knows no limit to its efficacy.

There is no limit in respect of the work done or the diminishment undergone, because we can always sink ourselves deeper into the perfecting of work to be achieved, or into the better utilization of distressing events. We can always be more industrious, more meticulous, more flexible . . .

Nor is there any limit in respect of the intention which animates our effort to act or to accept, because we can always go further in the interior perfecting of our conformity. There can always be greater detachment. Always greater love.

[117] Cf. Jn 4.34.

And there is no limit, indeed there is even less limit, in respect of the divine object in the ever-closer espousal of which our being can joyfully wear itself away. This is the moment to abandon all conception of static adherence. It can only be inadequate. And let us remember this: God does not offer himself to our finite beings as a thing all complete and ready to be embraced. For us he is eternal discovery and eternal growth. The more we think we understand him, the more he reveals himself as otherwise. The more we think we hold him, the further he withdraws, drawing us into the depths of himself. The nearer we approach him through all the efforts of nature and grace, the more he increases, in one and the same movement, his attraction over our powers, and the receptivity of our powers to that divine attraction.

Thus the privileged point which was mentioned a moment ago—the one point at which, for each one of us, at any moment, the divine milieu may be born, is not a fixed point in the universe. It is a moving center which we have to follow, like the magi their star.[118]

That star leads each one of us differently, one way or the other, in accordance with our vocation. But all the paths which it indicates have this in common: that they lead always upwards. (We have already said these things more than once, but it is important to group them together for the last time in the same bundle.) In any existence, if it has fidelity, greater desires follow on lesser ones, renunciation gradually gains mastery over pleasure, death consummates life. Finally the general drift throughout creation will have been the same for all. Sometimes through detachment of mind and spirit, sometimes through effective detachment, fidelity leads us all, more or less fast and more or less far, towards the same zone of minimal egoism and minimal pleasure—to where, for the more ecstatic creature, the divine light glows with greater amplitude and greater limpidity, beyond the intermediaries which have been, not rejected, but outstripped.

---

[118] Cf. Mt 2.1–2.

Purity, faith and fidelity—under the converging action of these three rays, the world melts and folds.

Like a huge fire that is fed by what should normally extinguish it, or like a mighty torrent which is swelled by the very obstacles placed to stem it, so the tension engendered by the encounter between human beings and God dissolves, bears along and volatilizes created things and makes them all, equally, serve the cause of union.

Joys, advances, sufferings, setbacks, faults, works, prayers, beauties, the powers of heaven, earth and hell—everything bows down under the touch of the heavenly waves; and everything yields up the portion of positive energy contained within its nature to contribute to the richness of the divine milieu.

Like the jet of flame that effortlessly pierces the hardest metal, so the spirit drawn to God penetrates through the world and makes its way enveloped in the luminous vapors of what it sublimates with him.

It does not destroy things, nor distort them; but it liberates them, directs them, transfigures them, animates them. It does not leave them behind but, as it rises, it leans on them for support; and carries along with it the chosen part in things.

Purity, faith and fidelity, static virtues and operative virtues, you are truly, in your serenity, nature's noblest energies—those which give even the material world its final consistency and its ultimate shape. You are the formative principles of the New Earth. Through you, threefold aspect of a same trusting adoration, 'we shall overcome the world': 'Hæc est victoria quæ vincit mundum fides nostra' (*'And this is the victory that conquers the world, our faith'*).[119]

C. *Collective progress in the divine milieu:*
the communion of saints and charity

1. *Preliminary remarks on the 'individual' value of the divine milieu*

In the foregoing pages we have been concerned in practice with the establishment and progress of the divine milieu in a soul

---

[119] 1 Jn 5.4.

envisaged as alone in the world in the presence of God. 'But what about its relationship to other people?' more than one reader must have thought; 'where do other people come in? What kind of christianity is this, that thinks it can build up an edifice without regard to love of neighbor?'

Our neighbors, as will now be seen, have an essential place in the edifice whose general outline we have tried to trace. But before we could insert them within its structure, we had to deal thoroughly with the problem of the 'divinization of the world' in the case of one or more individuals in particular; and this for two reasons.

In the first place, for reasons of method: because, by sound scientific rules, the study of particular cases must precede an attempt at generalization.

And in the second place, for reasons of nature: because no matter what extraordinary solidarity we have with each other in our development and in our consummation *in Christo Iesu*,[120] we all form natural units charged with our own responsibilities and our own incommunicable possibilities within that consummation. It is we who save ourselves or lose ourselves.

It was all the more important to stress this christian doctrine of individual salvation precisely as the perspectives developed here became more unitary and more universalist. It must never be forgotten that, as in the experiential spheres of the world, each individual, though enveloped within the same universe as all other individuals, presents an independent center of perspective and activity for that universe (so that there are as many partial universes as there are individuals), so in the domain of heavenly realities, however deeply impregnated we may be by the same creative and redemptive force, each one of us constitutes a particular center of divinization (so that there are as many partial divine milieus as there are christian souls).

Individuals, as we know, according to the dimness or excellence of their senses and intelligence, react so differently in the same

---

[120] Rom 3.24.

circumstances and in the presence of the same opportunities of perception and action, that if *per impossibile* we could migrate from one consciousness into another we should each time change our world. In the same way, God presents and gives himself to our souls under the same temporal and spatial 'species', but with very different degrees of reality and fullness, according to the faith, fidelity, and purity which his influence encounters. An achievement or a disaster which involves a whole group of people has as many different facets, finalities, and 'souls' as there are individuals involved: blind, absurd, indifferent or material to those who do not love and do not believe, it will be luminous, providential, charged with meaning and love to those who have succeeded in seeing and touching God everywhere. There are as many super-animations by God of secondary causes as there are forms of human trust and human fidelity. Although essentially single in its influx, providence is pluralized when in contact with us—just as a ray of sunlight takes on color or loses itself in the depths of the body which it strikes. The universe has many different storeys and many different compartments: *'in eadem domo, multæ mansiones'* ('In My Father's house are many mansions').[121]

That is why, in repeating over our lives the words the priest says over the bread and wine before the consecration, we should pray, each one of us, that the world may be transfigured for our use; *'ut nobis Corpus et Sanguis fiat D.N. Iesu Christi'* ('that they may become for us the body and blood of our Lord Jesus Christ').[122]

That is the first step. Before considering others (and to be able to do so) believers must make sure of their own personal sanctification—not out of egoism, but with a firm and broad understanding that the task of each one of us is to divinize the whole world in an infinitesimal and incommunicable degree.

We have tried to show how this partial divinization is possible. It only remains for us to integrate the elemental phenomenon and see

---

[121] Jn 14.2 (NKJ).

[122] Cf. *'ut nobis Corpus et Sanguis fiant Domini nostri Iesu Christi'* ['that they may become for us the body and blood of our Lord Jesus Christ'] (Eucharistic Prayer II, Roman Rite).

how the total divine milieu is formed by the confluence of our individual divine milieus, and how, to complete them, it reacts in its turn upon the particular destinies which it clasps in its embrace. The time has come to generalize our conclusions by multiplying them to infinity by the action of charity.

2. Intensification of the divine milieu through charity

To measure and understand the power of divinization contained in love for our neighbor, we must re-examine some of the themes already considered, and especially those passages in which we discussed the total unity of the eucharistic consecration.

Through the immensity of time and the disconcerting multiplicity of individuals, one single operation is taking place: the annexation to Christ of his elect—one single thing is being made: the Mystical Body of Christ, starting from all the sketchy spiritual powers scattered throughout the world. 'Hoc est Corpus meum' ('This is my body').[123] Nobody in the world can save us, or lose us, despite ourselves; that is true. But it is also true that our salvation is not pursued or achieved except in solidarity with the justification of the whole 'body of the elect'. In a real sense, only one person will be saved: Christ, the head and living embodiment of humanity. Each one of the elect is called upon to see God face to face. But this act of vision will be vitally inseparable from the elevating and illuminating action of Christ. In heaven we ourselves shall contemplate God, but, as it were, through the eyes of Christ.

If this is so, then our individual mystical effort awaits an essential completion in its union with the mystical effort of everyone else. The divine milieu which will ultimately be one in the Pleroma, must begin to become one during the earthly phase of our existence. So that although christians who hunger to live in God may have attained all possible purity of desire, faith in prayer, and fidelity in action, the divinization of their universe is still open to vast possibilities. It would still remain for them to link their elemental work to that of all

---

[123] Mt 26.26; Mk 14.22; Lk 22.19; 1 Cor 11.24. Words of consecration in the Eucharist.

the workers who surround them. The innumerable partial worlds which envelop the diverse human monads press in upon them from all around. Their task is to re-kindle their own ardor by contact with the ardor of all these focuses, to make their own sap communicate with the sap circulating in the other cells, to receive or propagate movement and life for the common benefit, and to adapt themselves to the common temperature and tension.

To what power is it reserved to burst asunder the envelopes in which our individual microcosms tend jealously to isolate themselves and vegetate? To what force is it given to merge and exalt our partial rays into the principal radiance of Christ?

To charity, the beginning and the end of all spiritual relationships. Christian charity, which is preached so fervently by the Gospels, is nothing else than the more or less conscious cohesion of souls engendered by their common convergence *in Christo Iesu*.[124] It is impossible to love Christ without loving others (as these others move towards Christ); and it is impossible to love others (in a spirit of broad human communion) without moving nearer to Christ. From now on, automatically, by a kind of living determinism, the individual divine milieus, as they establish themselves, tend to fuse with one another; and in this association they find a boundless increase of their ardor. This inevitable conjunction of forces has always been manifested, in the interior lives of the saints, by an overflowing love for everything which, in creatures, carries in itself a germ of eternal life. We have already examined 'the tension of communion' and its wonderful efficacy for directing us towards our human duty. It enables us to extract life even from powers which seem most heavily charged with death, and its ultimate effect is to precipitate christians into the love of souls.

Those with a passionate sense of the divine milieu cannot bear to find things about them obscure, tepid, and empty, things which should be full and vibrant with God. They are paralyzed by the thought of the innumerable spirits which are linked to theirs in the

---

[124] Rom 3.24.

unity of the same world, but are not yet fully kindled by the flame of the divine presence. They had thought for a time that they had only to stretch out their own hands to touch God to the measure of their desires. They now see that the only human embrace capable of worthily enfolding the divine is that of all men and women opening their arms to call down and welcome the Fire. The only subject ultimately capable of mystical transfiguration is the whole group of humanity forming a single body and a single soul in charity.

And this coalescence of the spiritual units of creation under the attraction of Christ is the supreme victory of faith over the world.

I confess, my God, that I have long been, and even now am, recalcitrant to the love of neighbor. Just as much as I have derived intense joy in the superhuman delight of dissolving myself and losing myself in the souls for which I was destined by the mysterious affinities of human love, so I have always felt an inborn hostility to, and closed myself to, the common run of those whom you tell me to love. I find no difficulty in integrating into my interior life everything above and beneath me (in the same line as me, as it were) in the universe—whether matter, plants, animals; and then powers, dominions and angels: these I accept without difficulty and delight to feel myself sustained within their hierarchy. But 'others', my God— by which I do not mean 'the poor, the halt, the lame and the sick', but 'others' quite simply as 'others', those who seem to exist independently of me because their universe seems closed to mine, and who seem to shatter the unity and the silence of the world for me—would I be sincere if I did not confess that my instinctive reaction is to rebuff them? and that the mere thought of entering into spiritual communication with them disgusts me?

Grant, O God, that the light of your countenance may shine for me in the life of these 'others'. The irresistible light of your eyes shining in the depth of things has already guided me towards all the work I must accomplish, and all the difficulties I must pass through. Grant that I may see you, even and above all, in the souls of my brothers and sisters, at their most personal, and most true, and most distant.

The gift which you call on me to make to these brothers and sisters—the only gift which my heart can make—is not the overwhelming tenderness of those specially privileged affections which you have placed in our lives as the most potent created factor of our interior growth, but something less sweet, but just as real, and more strong. Between myself and others, and with the help of your Eucharist, you want the fundamental attraction (which is already dimly felt in all love, if it is strong) to be made manifest—what mystically transforms the myriad of rational creatures into a kind of single monad in you, Jesus Christ. You want me to be drawn towards 'others', not by simple personal sympathy, but by what is much higher: the united affinities of a world for itself, and of that world for God.

You do not ask for the psychologically impossible—since what I am asked to cherish in the vast and unknown crowd is never anything save one and the same personal being which is yours.

Nor do you call for any hypocritical protestations of love for neighbor, because—since my heart cannot reach your person except at the depths of all that is most individually and concretely personal in every 'other'—it is to 'others' themselves, and not to some vague entity around them, that my charity is addressed.

No, you do not ask anything false or unattainable of me. You merely, through your revelation and your grace, force what is most human in me to become conscious of itself at last. Humanity was sleeping—it is still sleeping—imprisoned in the narrow joys of its little closed loves. A tremendous spiritual power is slumbering in the depths of our multitude, which will manifest itself only when we have learnt to break down the barriers of our egoisms and, by a fundamental recasting of our outlook, raise ourselves up to the habitual and practical vision of universal realities.

Jesus, Savior of human activity to which you have given meaning, Savior of human suffering to which you have given living value, be also the Savior of human unity; compel us to discard our pettinesses, and to venture forth, resting upon you, into the uncharted oceans of charity.

3. Outer darkness and the lost souls

The history of the Kingdom of God is, directly, one of a reunion. The total divine milieu is formed by the incorporation of every elected spirit in Jesus Christ. But to say 'elect' is to imply a choice, a selection. We should not be looking at the universal action of Jesus from a fully christian point of view if it were seen merely as a center

109

of attraction and beatification. It is precisely because he is the one who unites that he is also the one who separates and judges. The Gospels speak of the good seed, the sheep, the right hand of the Son of Man, the wedding feast and the fire that kindles joy. But there are also the tares, the goats, the left hand of the Judge, the closed door, the exterior darkness; and, at the antipodes of the fire that unites in love, there is the fire that destroys in isolation. The whole process out of which the New Earth is gradually born is an aggregation underlaid by a segregation.

In the foregoing pages (solely concerned with rising towards the divine focus and with offering ourselves more completely to its rays) our eyes have been systematically turned towards the light, though we have never ceased to feel the darkness and the void beneath us— the rarefication or absence of God over which our path has been suspended. But this inferior darkness, which we sought to flee, could equally well have been a kind of abyss opening on to sheer non-being. Imperfection, sin, evil, the flesh, appeared to us mainly as a retrograde step, a reverse aspect of things, which ceased to exist for us the further we penetrated into God.

Your revelation, O Lord, compels me to believe more. The powers of evil, in the universe, are not only an attraction, a deviation, a minus sign, an annihilating return to plurality. In the course of the spiritual evolution of the world, certain conscious elements in it, certain monads, deliberately detached themselves from the mass that is stimulated by your attraction. Evil has become incarnate in them, has been 'substantialized' in them. And now I am surrounded by dark presences, by evil beings, by malign things, intermingled with your luminous presence. That separated whole constitutes a definitive loss, an immortal wastage from the genesis of the world. There is not only inferior darkness; there is also exterior darkness. That is what the Gospels tell us.

Of the mysteries which we have to believe, O Lord, there is none, without a doubt, which so affronts our human views as that of damnation. And the more human we become, that is, conscious of the treasures hidden in the least of beings and of the value represented by the smallest atom in the final unity, the more lost we feel at the thought of hell. We could perhaps understand falling back into inexistence . . . but what are we to make of eternal uselessness and eternal suffering?

You have told me, O God, to believe in hell. But you have forbidden me to hold with absolute certainty that any single person has been damned. I shall therefore make no attempt to consider the damned here, nor even to discover—by whatsoever means—whether there are any. I shall accept the existence of hell on your word, as a structural element in the universe, and I shall pray and meditate until that awe-inspiring thing appears to me as a strengthening and even blessed complement to the vision of your omnipresence which you have opened out to me.

And in truth, Lord, there is no need for me to force either my mind or things to perceive a source of life even in the mystery of that second death. We do not have to peer very closely into that exterior darkness to discover in it a greater tension and a further deepening of your greatness.

I know that the powers of evil, considered in their deliberate and malign action, can do nothing to trouble the divine milieu around me. As they try to penetrate into my universe, their influence (if I have enough faith) suffers the fate common to all created energy; caught up and twisted round by your irresistible energy, temptations and evils are converted into good, and fan the fires of love.

I know, too, that considered from the point of view of the void created by their defection from the Mystical Body, the fallen spirits cannot detract from the perfection of the Pleroma. Each soul that is lost in spite of the call of grace ought to spoil the perfection of the final and general union; but instead, O God, you offset it by one of those recastings which restore the universe at every moment to a new freshness and a new purity. The damned are not excluded from the Pleroma, but only from its luminous aspect, and from its beatification. They lose it, but they are not lost to it.

The existence of hell, then, does not destroy anything and does not spoil anything in the divine milieu whose progress all around me I have followed with delight. I can even feel, moreover, that it effects something great and new there. It adds an accent, a gravity, a contrast, a depth which would not exist without it. The peak can only be measured from the abyss which it crowns.

I was speaking a moment or two ago—looking at things from a human point of view—of a universe closed, from below, by non-being, that is, of a scale of magnitudes that somehow stops dead at zero. But now, O God, tearing open the inferior darkness of the universe, you show me that there is another hemisphere at my feet—the very real domain, descending without end, of existences which are, at least, possible.

Does the reality of this negative pole of the world not double the immensity and the urgency of power with which you come upon me?

O Jesus, our splendidly beautiful and jealous Master, closing my eyes to what my human weakness cannot as yet understand and therefore cannot bear—that is, to the reality of the damned—I desire at least to make the ever present threat of damnation a part of my habitual and practical vision of the world, not to fear you, but to be more intensely yours.

Just now I besought you, Jesus, to be not only a brother for me,—but a God. Now, invested as you are with the redoubtable power of selection which places you at the summit of the world as the principle of universal attraction and universal repulsion, you truly appear to me as the immense and living force which I was seeking everywhere that I might adore it: the fires of hell and the fires of heaven are not two different forces, but contrary manifestations of the same energy.

I pray, O Master, that the flames of hell may touch neither me nor any of those whom I love . . . I pray, my God, that they may never touch anyone (and I know that you will forgive this bold prayer); but that, for each and every one of us, their somber glow may add, together with all the abysses that they reveal, to the blazing plenitude of the divine milieu.

112

EPILOGUE
Awaiting the Parousia

Segregation and aggregation: separation of the evil elements of the world, and 'co-adunation'[125] of the elemental worlds that the faithful spirits construct around them in work and pain. Under the influence of this twofold movement, which is still almost entirely hidden, the universe is being transformed and is maturing all around us.

We are sometimes inclined to think that the same things are monotonously repeated over and over again in the history of creation. That is because the season is too long by comparison with the brevity of our individual lives, and the transformation too vast and too interior by comparison with our superficial and restricted outlook, for us to see the progress of what is tirelessly taking place in and through all matter and all spirit. Let us believe in Revelation, our faithful support (once again) in our most human forebodings. Under the commonplace envelope of things and of all our purified and salvaged efforts, the new earth is being slowly engendered.

One day, the Gospels tell us, the tension gradually accumulating between humanity and God will touch the limits prescribed by the possibilities of the world. And then will come the end. Then the presence of Christ, which has been silently accruing in things, will suddenly be revealed—like a flash of light from pole to pole. Breaking through all the barriers within which the veil of matter and the watertightness of souls have seemingly kept it confined, it will invade the face of the earth. And, under the final-liberated action of the true affinities of being, the spiritual atoms of the world will be

---

[125] Lit. 'co-union'.

borne along by a force generated by the powers of cohesion proper to the universe itself, and will occupy, whether within Christ or without Christ (but always under the influence of Christ), the place of happiness or pain designated for them by the living structure of the Pleroma. *'Sicut fulgur exit ab Oriente et para usque in Occidentem . . . Sicut venit diluvium et tulit omnes . . . Ita erit adventus Filii hominis'* ('For as the lightning comes from the east and flashes as far as the west, so will be the coming of the Son of Man').[126] Like lightning, like a conflagration, like a flood, the attraction exerted by the Son of Man will lay hold of all the whirling elements in the universe to reunite them or subject them to his body. *'Ubicumque fuerit corpus illuc congregabuntur aquilæ'* ('Wherever the corpse is, there the vultures will gather').[127]

Such will be the consummation of the divine milieu.

As the Gospels warn us, it would be vain to speculate as to the hour and the modalities of this formidable event. But we have to expect it.

Expectation—anxious, collective and operative expectation of an end of the world, that is, of an issue for the world—is perhaps the supreme christian function and the most distinctive characteristic of our religion.

Historically speaking, that expectation has never ceased to guide the progress of our faith like a torch. The Israelites were constantly 'expectant',—and the first christians too. Christmas, which might have been thought to turn our gaze towards the past, has only fixed it further in the future. The Messiah, who appeared for a moment in our midst, only allowed himself to be seen and touched for a moment before vanishing once again, more luminous and ineffable than ever, into the depths of the future. He came. Yet now we must expect him—no longer a small chosen group among us, but all people—once again and more than ever. The Lord Jesus will only come soon

---

[126] The exact wording of the Vulgate is: *'Sicut enim fulgur exit ab oriente et paret usque in occidente ita erit et adventus Filii hominis'* ['For as the lightning comes from the east and flashes as far as the west, so will be the coming of the Son of Man'] (Mt 24.27).
[127] *'Ubicumque fuerit corpus illuc congregabuntur aquilæ'* (Mt 24.28).

if we ardently expect him. It is an accumulation of desires that should cause the Parousia to burst upon us.

Successors to Israel, we christians have been charged with keeping the flame of desire ever alive in the world. Only twenty centuries have passed since the Ascension. What have we made of our expectancy?

A rather childish haste, combined with the error in perspective which led the first generation of christians to believe in the immediate return of Christ, has unfortunately left us disillusioned and suspicious. Our faith in the Kingdom of God has been disconcerted by the resistance of the world to good. A certain pessimism, perhaps, encouraged by an exaggerated conception of the original fall, has led us to regard the world as decidedly and incorrigibly wicked . . . And so we have allowed the flame to die down in our sleeping hearts. No doubt we see with greater or less distress the approach of individual death. No doubt, again, our prayers and actions are conscientiously directed to bringing about 'the coming of the Kingdom of God'. But in fact how many of us are genuinely moved in the depths of our hearts by the wild hope that our earth will be recast? Who is there who sets a course in the midst of our darkness towards the first glimmer of a real dawn? Where are the christians in whom the impatient longing for Christ succeeds, not in submerging (as it should) the cares of human love and human interests, but even in counterbalancing them? Where are the catholics as passionately vowed (by conviction and not by convention) to spreading the hopes of the Incarnation as are many humanitarians to spreading the dream of the new City? We persist in saying that we keep vigil in expectation of the master. But in reality we should have to admit, if we were sincere, that we no longer expect anything.

The flame must be revived at all costs. At all costs we must renew in ourselves the desire and the hope for the great Coming. But where are we to look for the source of this rejuvenation? We shall clearly find it, first and foremost, in an increase of the attraction exercised directly by Christ upon his members. And then in an increase of the interest, discovered by our thought, in the preparation and consummation of the Parousia. And from where is this interest itself to spring? From the perception of a more intimate connection between the victory of Christ and the outcome of the work which our human effort below is seeking to construct.

We constantly forget that the supernatural is a ferment, a soul, and not a complete organism. Its role is to transform 'nature'; but it cannot do so apart from the matter which nature provides it with. If the Jewish people have remained turned towards the Messiah for three thousand years, it is because he appeared to them to enshrine the glory of their people. If the disciples of S. Paul lived in perpetual expectation of the great day, that was because it was to the Son of Man that they looked for a personal and tangible solution to the problems and the injustices of life. The expectation of heaven cannot remain alive unless it is incarnate. What body shall we give to ours today?

That of a huge and totally human hope. Let us look at the earth around us. What is happening under our eyes within the mass of peoples? What is the cause of this disorder in society, this uneasy agitation, these swelling waves, these whirling and mingling currents, and these turbulent and formidable new impulses? Humanity is visibly passing through a crisis of growth. Humanity is becoming dimly aware of its shortcomings and its capacities. And as we said on the first page, it sees the universe growing luminous like the horizon just before sunrise. It has a sense of premonition and of expectation.

Subject, like everyone else, to that attraction, christians, we said, sometimes wonder, and are uneasy. May they not be bestowing their adoration on an idol?

Our study, now completed, of the divine milieu suggests an answer to this fear.

Those of us who are disciples of Christ must not hesitate to harness this force, which needs us, and which we need. On the contrary, under pain of allowing it to be lost and of perishing ourselves, we should share those aspirations, in essence religious, which make the men and women of today feel so strongly the immensity of the world, the greatness of the mind, and the sacred

116

value of every new truth. It is in this way that our christian generation will learn again to anticipate the joy of expectation.

We have gone deeply into these new perspectives: the progress
of the universe, and especially of the human universe, does not take
place in competition with God, nor does it squander energies that
we rightly owe to him. The greater we humans become, the more
humanity becomes united, with consciousness of, and mastery of, its
potentialities, the more beautiful creation will be, the more perfect
adoration will become, and the more Christ will find, for mystical
extensions, a body worthy of resurrection. The world can no more
have two summits than a circumference can have two centers. The
star for which the world is waiting, without yet being able to give it
a name, or rightly appreciate its true transcendence, or even recognize the most spiritual and divine of its rays, is, necessarily, Christ
himself, in whom we hope. To desire the Parousia, all we have to do
is to let the very heart of the earth, as we christianize it, beat within
us.

Why then, O people of little faith, do you fear or repudiate the
progress of the world? Why foolishly multiply your warnings and
your prohibitions? 'Don't venture . . . Don't try . . . everything is
known: the earth is empty and old; there is nothing more to be
discovered.'

We must try everything for Christ! We must hope everything for
Christ! *'Nihil intentatum!'* ('Leave nothing unattempted!') That, on the
contrary, is the true christian attitude. To divinize does not mean to
destroy, but to super-create. We shall never know all that the
Incarnation still expects of the world's potentialities. We shall never
put enough hope in the growing unity of humanity.

Lift up your head, O Jerusalem. Look at the immense crowds of
those who build and those who seek. All over the world, men and
women are toiling—in laboratories, in studios, in deserts, in facto-
ries, in the vast social crucible. The ferment that is taking place by
their instrumentality in art and science and thought is happening for
your sake. Open, then, your arms and your heart, like your Lord
Jesus, and welcome the waters, the flood and the sap of humanity.

117

Accept it, this sap—for, without its baptism, you will wither, without desire, like a flower out of water; tend it, since, without your sun, it will disperse itself wildly in sterile shoots.

The temptations of too large a world, the seductions of too beautiful a world—where are these now?

They do not exist.

Now the earth can certainly clasp me in her giant arms. She can swell me with her life, or take me back into her dust. She can deck herself out for me with every charm, with every horror, with every mystery. She can intoxicate me with her perfume of tangibility and unity. She can cast me to my knees in expectation of what is maturing in her breast.

But her enchantments can no longer do me harm, since she has become for me, over and above herself, the body of the one who is and of the one who comes!

The divine milieu.[128]

Tientsin
November 1926–March 1927

---

[128] 'It is a long time now since I tried, in "The Mass on the World" and "The Divine Milieu", to express the admiration and amazement I felt in the face of perspectives as yet hardly formulated within me.

'Today, after forty years of continuous reflection, it is still exactly the same fundamental vision which I sense I must present, and share with others, in its mature form—for the last time. With less exuberance and freshness of expression, perhaps, than at the moment of our first encounter, but always with the same wonder—and the same passion' ('Le Christique' (1955), Le Cœur de la matière, Seuil, 1976, pp. 97–8 (our translation); cf. 'The Christic' (1955), The Heart of Matter, Collins, 1978, p. 83).

No work of this great believer can be understood except as an expression of this 'fundamental vision' of the divine milieu—the vision (always implied even when not explicitly stated) of Christ as 'all in all', of the universe moved and com-penetrated by God in the totality of its evolution. This book illuminates to the full the vision that is to be found in The Human Phenomenon. (French Editor's Note.)

INDEX

119

Pierre Teilhard de Chardin
(1881–1955)

Sussex Academic Press, in a project endorsed by Editions de Seuil, the Teilhard Fondation (Paris), and the British Teilhard Association, intend to publish new English-language translations of all of Teilhard's works. They will be divided into four volumes—Mysticism, Science, Praxis, and Faith—comprising twelve books.

COLLECTED WORKS BY THEME

Mysticism
The Divine Milieu
Writings in the Time of War
The Heart of the Matter

Science
The Phenonomenon of Man
[The Human Phenomenon]
The Appearance of Man
The Vision of the Past
Man's Place in Nature
[The Human Zoological Group]

Praxis
The Future of Man
Human Energy
Activation of Energy
Toward the Future

Faith
Science and Christ
Christianity and Evolution

All books will contain introductions by leading scholars, who will put Teilhard's writings in a more current context than their original publications. Publishing information, including *The Teilhard Lexicon: Understanding the Language, Terminology and Vision of the Writings of Pierre Teilhard de Chardin*, by Siôn Cowell ("Provides great assistance in deciphering Teilhard's terminology and interpreting his thought. Extremely friendly to the user," *Choice*), is detailed on the Sussex Academic website www.sussex-academic.co.uk

Readers interested in Teilhardian studies are invited to contact
THE BRITISH TEILHARD ASSOCIATION
12 Falconer's Field, Harpenden AL5 3ES
secretary@teilhard.org.uk

THE AMERICAN TEILHARD ASSOCIATION (ATA)
Department of Religion, Bucknell University,
701 Moore Avenue, Lewisburg, PA 17837, USA